OPENING
SPACE

A VISION FOR FRESH EXPRESSIONS
OF CHURCH AND CREATIVE MISSION

SHANNON KISER

Cover design and layout by Nate Farro
Page design and layout by PerfecType, Nashville, Tennessee

Kiser, Shannon
  Opening space : a vision for fresh expressions of church and creative mission / Shannon Kiser. – Franklin, Tennessee : Seedbed Publishing, ©2025.

  pages ; cm.

  ISBN 9798888001301 (paperback)
  ISBN 9798888001318 (ePub)
  ISBN 9798888001325 (uPDF)
  OCLC 1513519082

  1. Church--21st century. 2. Church work--21st century.
  3. Christian life--21st century 4. Public worship--Christianity.
  5. Christian communities. I. Title.

BV600.3 .K5737 2025   262.001/7   2025935256

SEEDBED PUBLISHING
Franklin, Tennessee
seedbed.com

CONTENTS

PREFACE

I am endlessly marveling at God's unfolding story that has, at its core, the radical grace and unconditional love of a God made known to us in Jesus Christ, a story that continues its arc toward God's promise to renew all things. I'm grateful for the opportunity to play a miniscule part in that story, though I could never have written the script in which I find myself. When I was in seminary, Mission and Evangelism was my least engaging course, and I pictured myself as a pastor in a beautiful sanctuary with a bustling congregation. Thirty years later, the heart of my ministry is mission and evangelism, and the church that I serve is best known for its bustling coffee shop and community impact.

Two decades ago, a single question began to reshape my ministry: *How might our church become more connected to the community around us?* This question changed everything. While I still cherish the grandeur of hymns and the sacredness of traditional church spaces, I've come to realize the deep joy and gratitude that comes from witnessing God at work in the everyday spaces of my community.

Over the last ten years, I have had the immense privilege of walking alongside my brothers and sisters at Riverside Presbyterian Church as we pursued a radical vision. Together, we partnered with a title company to purchase half of an office building, fully entering into the daily life of our city and living out radical hospitality through a seven-day-a-week coffee shop. This coffee shop, complete with an indoor children's play area, has become a natural gathering space for our diverse community. It's in this coffee shop where I've had some of the most profound spiritual conversations of my ministry—often with people who might never have stepped into our worship service. This mission has been both messy and beautiful, and every time I connect with someone's story, I am reminded of how God can do *far more* than we could ever ask or imagine (Eph. 3:20).

In the past decade, I've also had the honor of coaching leaders who have followed God's Spirit into similarly creative new ventures—forming new faith communities in places like community gardens, soup kitchens, fitness centers, parks, cafés, and art studios. These efforts have opened the door for artists, recovering addicts, young people, athletes, individuals with disabilities, and outdoor enthusiasts to experience the transforming power of the gospel in shared community.

I am convinced that the future of the church lies in a dual embrace: the richness and beauty of the existing church with its sanctuaries, preachers, and musicians, and the creative, innovative efforts that embody and bear witness to the gospel beyond the walls of the church, right among the everyday lives of people. It is with this conviction that I've written this book. My hope is that you, too, can experience the incredible joy and transformation that comes as we join in God's mission, both in the steeples and in the streets.

INTRODUCTION

When Did Church Become Something We Go To?

The Gospels are filled with accounts of Jesus revealing, describing, and explaining what abundant life looks like in the kingdom of God. He spoke about the kingdom of God, his life modeled the kingdom of God, and his actions revealed the kingdom of God. People flocked to him because he welcomed the unwelcome and breathed life into the lifeless.

Along the way, Jesus invited his disciples to immerse themselves into villages and towns to share this reality with others. He wanted to teach his disciples how to help others experience God's kingdom—a kingdom pulsing with kindness, brimming with hope, animated by justice, and saturated with the presence of Jesus.

Jesus's death on the cross revealed the lengths that he would go to communicate the depths of God's love for us and dismantle anything that would separate us from God's love. Jesus's resurrection provided a way for people from all walks of life—and even throughout all time— to join him in this kingdom way of life. But not just for themselves. It was always meant to be shared with others.

Have you ever noticed that when Jesus returns to heaven, he doesn't leave his followers with a religious system or a marketing plan? He leaves a *community* who has tasted the goodness of God's kingdom and who is committed to the way of Jesus.

Not only that, he leaves this community *with a mission*, empowered by the Holy Spirit, to introduce Jesus and God's kingdom to the world as they live grateful lives at work, at school, at home, and in rhythms of every day.

This is what it means to be the church.

If you've ever thought, *There's got to be more to the Christian life than this*, then maybe it's time to go back to what Jesus had in mind when he gave his community their purpose.

Go.

Love God and love others.

Make disciples.

And I will be with you.

This is what fresh expressions are all about.

A Vision for the Church

Luke's gospel tells the story of a group of friends who deeply desired for their paralyzed friend to encounter Jesus. For so long this friend's life had been marked with hardship and sorrow, with no way to work, no way to enter the temple, and no end in sight. Helpless, they watched as their friend began to lose hope and withdraw into the crevices of isolation and desperation. But they had not forgotten him. They wouldn't turn their back on him. Their hope swelled as they heard about this Jesus who was captivatingly different and curiously powerful. He was touching the untouchables, healing the impossible, and speaking life into what was lifeless. What might be possible if they could get their friend into Jesus's presence?

Blocked from the door, they tried and tried to get their friend into the room with Jesus, but every which way, they were obstructed. Do you ever feel this way sometimes? Have you ever wanted a friend to discover the joy of life in Jesus, but didn't know how to help them do so? How often do we just shrug and say, "Oh well," and move on with our regular routines?

But love for this friend would not let them give up.

Can you imagine the desperate conversation that led them to consider the roof as a creative alternative?

Can you conjure up the sheer determination that it took to lower this paralyzed man through the roof to the feet of Jesus?

And can you imagine the joy that surged through them as they watched their friend healed right in front of them?

There were crowds of people in that room who were amazed by what they heard and saw. There was a group of friends who were forever changed in the presence of Jesus. As I think about the church today, I wonder what would break loose if our Sunday morning crowd became amazed at Jesus once again. I wonder how many little micro-communities of friends not currently in our pews could experience the amazing things Jesus wants to do in and through them. This is the vision for fresh expressions.

The Need for Change

Church leaders across the denominational landscape are recognizing that something fundamental must change. Mainline leaders look out at aging congregations and realize they can't continue the way they always have. Even vibrant congregations are rethinking what needs to shift to be able to embrace a more faithful way of being church in the twenty-first century. Megachurches, despite investing millions of dollars into new campuses, are wondering whether this is the best way to steward their resources for the sake of the gospel. The numbers of "Nones" and "Dones"—those who have no church connection or who no longer desire to maintain any church connection—is skyrocketing in North America. Most church leaders are at a loss about what to do.

Recent statistics bear this out. According to data analyst Ryan Burge:

- 66 percent of churches are plateaued or declining[1]
- 93 million U.S. adults identify as "Nones"[2]
- "Nothing in particular" is the fastest growing religious group in America[3]
- There is no major denomination where a majority are under forty-five years old[4]

These are more than just statistics on a graph. Each data point reflects real people and real churches. Most importantly, they reflect countless people who will never experience the fullness of life that Jesus offers if we wait for them to come to our church buildings. While we busy ourselves preparing sermons and planning children's activities inside our church buildings, all around us are families longing for restoration, addicts desperate for healing, young people searching for purpose, and communities wondering if good news is actually possible in this crazy world.

Introducing Fresh Expressions

In this resource, we introduce an approach with a proven track record for connecting with this growing number of people that existing churches are struggling to engage. Fresh expressions are a viable path of outreach and evangelism for *every size church*. These efforts require no large budgets, no seminary degrees, and no expensive church growth consultants. Instead, they empower ordinary disciples in our congregations to start small Jesus-shaped communities in the everyday spaces and places of their lives. Through these communities, people are encountering the contagious goodness of Jesus, coming to faith, and forming church right where they are in the middle of everyday life.

As fresh expressions of church begin to take root, an abundant harvest is being unleashed.

Those who are starting these new Christian communities are finding their own walk with God transformed and deepened.

Those who once had no interest in church or church people are tasting the life of the gospel.

Congregations are increasing in spiritual vitality as they discover God's Spirit powerfully at work in the world beyond their church doors.

Fresh expressions are Christian communities emerging in diverse places and spaces all around the world. They come in various shapes and sizes, reflecting the cultures and settings they inhabit. Some are active, some more contemplative; some are innovative, some are ancient. We've seen them emerge on playgrounds, in prisons, on mountains, in cafés, and more. And it can happen in virtually any context, including yours. These simple communities are helping those who would have never walked into the door of a church building to encounter the love of God in Jesus Christ.

We want to be extremely clear: Fresh expressions are not replacing existing churches. Rather, this movement is expanding the church. And it is changing lives.

Do you want to get back to the heart of what Jesus started two thousand years ago?

Let us show you how.

Discussion Questions

1. What does it mean to you to "be" church rather than "go to" church?

2. How would you describe your existing church?

3. Who is it your church is not currently able to engage, no matter how great your worship or programs may be?

4. How might fresh expressions complement or enhance the life of your existing church?

A FRESH EXPRESSION STORY: PLAY N PRAY

A pastor and a church administrator walked onto a playground. This is not the beginning of a joke, but rather the beginning of a new Christian community. These women took their children to the playground one day as they committed to prayerfully inhabit the space while their children played. They watched their kids easily making friends with other kids on the playground, and found that they, too, were naturally meeting and connecting with other moms.

As they came back time and time again, they discovered the conversations were getting more honest about the joys and the struggles of the child-raising season of life, and as people discovered these two women were people of faith, it naturally opened space for people to begin to ask if they could pray for them. *If it is so easy to connect here,* they wondered, *why do we keep trying to get people into our building? Why can't we just form an expression of church right here?*

So that's what they did. Instead of just hoping they would run into these new friends at the playground, they chose a regular gathering time and invited anyone who wanted to join them with their kids at the playground to come for "Play N Pray." They offered snacks, playtime, faith conversation, and an intergenerational prayer time, recognizing this was such an easy way to connect with people. The children wanted to be there, but so did the parents.

This fresh expression experiment cost almost nothing—a few snacks and a hand-drawn yard sign. But the laughter, the fellowship, and the playful prayer time is giving these families a handhold to experience Christian faith in community in a place where they were already spending their free time. Jesus is still meeting people in the everyday spaces of life, and for Play N Pray, it is happening right in the middle of a community playground.

THE NEED

Why Do We Need Fresh Expressions?

One day, while [Jesus] was teaching, Pharisees and teachers of the law were sitting nearby . . . and the power of the Lord was with him to heal. Just then some men came, carrying a paralyzed man on a bed . . .

—LUKE 5:17–18

Paralyzed

When I was a child hitting puberty, doctors discovered I had a congenital condition causing me to slowly lose the function of my legs. Although my brain was telling my legs to move, they just weren't getting the message. If this trajectory continued, I would slowly become paralyzed. My parents faced a heart-wrenching decision that no parent wants to make: either take the risk and give the neurosurgeon permission to operate or let the symptoms continue to deteriorate my leg function. Having the surgery wouldn't guarantee a positive outcome. But not having the surgery would most certainly lead to full paralysis. It was a risk, but they chose the surgery out of love. Today, I marvel at the simple gift of being able to take a walk with my husband and my dog.

Reflecting on my journey, I wonder if there are parallels for the church to consider. We live in a world in need of healing. Some symptoms are acute: a pandemic, a changing climate, increasing economic disparity, poverty, violence, racism, polarization, mass shootings, and the deadliest drug overdose epidemic in U.S. history. Beneath the surface, subtler signs of disease persist: loneliness, cynicism, lack of meaning and purpose, hopelessness, regret, shame, disappointment, and restlessness.

Our church runs a coffee shop filled every day with people who look just fine on the outside. I am served by a barista paralyzed by indecision about his future. I see a lonely widower drinking his coffee by himself, paralyzed by loneliness. I glance at the businessman paralyzed by desperation to close this deal or lose his business. I see the patron still paralyzed by grief over her son's untimely death. I watch as the pressures of life in a frenetic culture spill over when a customer becomes agitated that her order is not ready. I encounter the seething anger of one customer who finds out this coffee shop is run by a church, and after being deeply wounded by church in his past, is adamant that not one dime of his will go to support a religion that has so deeply damaged him.

Jesus has the power to heal, but there is a disconnect between the Healer and our world today. The church, the body of Christ, is meant to partner with Jesus in the new creation and the healing of the world. Yet, the church has become the last place many will turn to for healing, meaning, and purpose. Congregations and church leaders lament the empty pews on Sunday mornings and are perhaps even paralyzed in their attempts to reach new generations. But the fact is, many people are not interested in pursuing a faith community after being disappointed, angered, and shamed by church people. Others simply find the church irrelevant, preferring other endeavors that feel more comfortable, interesting, or life-giving. Why join a church when your CrossFit group is far more encouraging and life-changing?

Try googling "Why are Christians so . . ." and see what comes up in your search. It may be no surprise that Google's suggestions include: mean, judgmental, hypocritical, angry, and boring. Is it any wonder why our congregations are declining, while at the same time, the spiritual longings of our culture are so raw?

Scripture tells us that when Jesus looked out at the people, "he had compassion for them, because they were harassed and helpless, like sheep without a shepherd" (Matt. 9:36). I believe that's how Jesus sees our twenty-first-century culture: harassed and helpless in many ways. Just as he was moved with compassion for the crowds on that hillside in Palestine, he is moved with compassion for you, your congregation, and the neighborhoods, needs, and networks that surround your church.

As a matter of fact, Jesus invites our congregations to share his heartbeat, to engage our increasingly paralyzed world with the hope and the heart and the healing of Jesus.

The question is: *Will we take the risk of moving out in love?*

Through fresh expressions, congregations are doing just that. Regular congregations like yours are reconnecting with people who have written off church. Everyday Christians are discovering the adventure of following Jesus into surprising and life-changing forms of community centered around Jesus and coming alive as disciples themselves as they do so.

Fresh expressions are new forms of church connecting with people right where they are: in cafés and yoga studios, on hiking trails and in kayaks, on disc golf courses and ball fields, in food pantries and recovery groups, around dinner tables and shared passions to make a difference in the world. In the metaverse and in the workplace, in urban settings and rural settings, in suburbs and small-town settings, the good news of Jesus is being experienced in all sorts of places among all sorts of people through expressions of Christian community that actually feel like good news to those who are encountering it. Fresh expressions are bringing the church that Jesus loves closer to the people that Jesus loves.

What Is a Fresh Expression?

A fresh expression is a form of church for our changing culture established primarily for the benefit of people who are not yet members of any church. It will come into being through principles of listening, friendship, service, incarnational mission, and making disciples. And it will have the potential to become a mature expression of church shaped by the gospel and the enduring marks of the church and for its cultural context.

- A fresh expression of church is not a temporary effort, like a summer mission trip or a community fall festival.
- It is not a tweak of what your church presently does, like the live streaming of your Sunday morning service or adding a young adult Bible study to your small-group portfolio.
- It is not a new, catchy title for one of your existing ministries.

It is taking a risk, in the way of an incarnational God, to enter into the lives of people right where they are, in the middle of the complexity and messiness of everyday life, and helping them to discover the joyful adventure of life with Jesus in Christian community. Paradoxically, that adventure will change you too.

Fresh expressions don't replace the existing, inherited church. It multiplies it.

The Characteristics of a Fresh Expression

Fresh expressions of church start with the compassion of Jesus. A Jesus-follower feels the stirring to give time, energy, and passion to a particular group of people, a particular place, or a particular need. A congregation catches the vision to encourage the everyday people in their pews to imagine what it could look like to be a missionary in the midst of the lives they already inhabit. Fresh expressions don't start with a fully formed program strategy and marketing plan; they grow out of a heart for people who God loves.

 Fresh expressions are *incarnational.* Just as Christ set aside the privileges of heaven, took on human flesh, and entered our world as a servant, the church is invited to follow in the footsteps of Jesus. Instead of staying in our Christian enclaves, we are invited to enter into our culture just as Jesus entered into our human world. Instead of seeking to gain power, we humbly listen, love, and serve, embodying the new creation that Jesus came to unleash into a world in need of healing. It is embracing risk, stepping out of what we know, and becoming vulnerable in the way of Jesus as we relate with people on their turf and on their terms.

 Fresh expressions are *missional.* We are sent out by God to love and serve and engage in mission among those not currently served by any church. Or as Jesus challenges his disciples: "As the Father sent me, so I am sending you" (John 20:21 NIV). It's not about storming our communities to take hostages for Jesus. It's about following Jesus who is already at work ahead of us in all the nooks and crannies of our communities, partnering with Jesus as good news people. As agents of mercy, compassion, and love, we are sent by Jesus to be present in these spaces, patiently loving and serving and helping the spiritually curious connect to the God who loves them.

 Fresh expressions are *contextual.* They take seriously the cultural context in which the mission is being formed. A Jesus-centered community forming with skateboarders in a skate park will look very different than a Jesus-centered community forming with single-parent families around dinner tables. Yet, they make perfect sense for the context in which they are emerging.

 Fresh expressions are *formational.* They help people enter more fully into the life of Christ and live as disciples. They are more than social clubs. They are more than service projects. The *way* they form disciples may look very different than discipleship in an existing, inherited congregation. But through mentorship, shared practices of the community, prayer, and God's Word, disciples are being formed.

 Fresh expressions are *ecclesial.* As they mature, these communities become more than just small-group Bible studies (as wonderful as those are!). They begin to evidence the enduring marks of the church, and the community itself begins to understand its identity as being part of the larger body of Christ. You'll begin to hear things like this: "This is my church!"

The Opportunity Before Us

We have a choice: Our churches can keep doing what we are doing and find ourselves increasingly paralyzed. Or we can embody the compassion of Jesus and take a risk and see what the power of the Lord can do both in us and through us.

An Emerging Movement

We have much to learn from the Global South, where there is literally an explosion of people coming to faith in Jesus. Their commitment to prayer, heart for community care, and zeal for evangelism has much to teach the North American church. But the Holy Spirit also seems to be doing something curious in the Western world. In 2004, the Church of England released a paper entitled "Mission-Shaped Church" as ecclesial leaders were becoming increasingly aware of something happening in their midst that was *not at all* a part of a larger institutional church strategy: New forms of church were inexplicably emerging and connecting with people that the existing cathedrals were not. While ever dwindling congregations were gathering in their parishes for Sunday morning worship, new communities were bubbling up in cafés and pubs, in parks and housing developments and refugee centers, led by primarily lay innovators who were willing to boldly follow Jesus into the nooks and crannies of their community. Instead of ignoring what God seemed to be doing, the institutional church found a way to recognize, bless, and encourage these newly forming communities, rediscovering this purpose in their historic church documents: "The Church of England . . . professes the faith uniquely revealed in the Holy Scriptures and set forth in the catholic creeds, which faith the Church is called up *to proclaim afresh in each generation.*"[5]

Thus, these Christian communities began to be known as fresh expressions. In an increasingly postmodern, multireligious, and nonreligious culture, fresh expressions were cultivating immersive kinds of experiences in the settings of everyday life. Here, communal life with Jesus was being transmitted to people who had not yet received it. The Church of England saw this as a work of the Holy Spirit and, from the onset of the Fresh Expressions movement, took a posture of multi-denominational, multi-national collaboration. Those of us in the North American context have the gift of learning from our brothers and sisters in England who have had a head start in navigating these post-Christian waters. As they have been learning from these emerging efforts, they have graciously been willing to share their learnings as we respond to similar shifts in our North American context.

How might God be inviting us to join in what seems to be a movement of the Holy Spirit for our time?

The narrative for too long now has been the decline of the institutional church in North America. But that's not the whole story. We live in an age of spiritual searching. In a time of waning trust in institutions, there is no lack of signs that people are longing for something beyond themselves. Go into any crystal shop or bookstore self-help section. Watch impromptu candlelight vigils spring up in the spaces of heartache and loss. I attended a traveling Burning Man art exhibit some years ago, and the Temple Room was replete with the longings and laments of people trying to give voice to the prayers inside of them when given a wood plank, a pen, and an invitation to be honest. The raw spiritual desperation was profound. People in this culture may be leaving the church, but they are not devoid of spiritual curiosity. Perhaps it's no surprise that the Holy Spirit is moving toward those longings with the characteristic grace and love of Jesus Christ.

As much as we love our churches, we are invited to grapple with the reality that many people in our communities just don't love our churches. But what if our churches loved them enough to join in what the Spirit already seems to be doing? Spiritual curiosity is on the rise . . . will we recognize it, and help new generations experience afresh the one who has the power to heal the deepest longings of their hearts?

Discussion Questions

1. How has your congregation felt stuck, or paralyzed, when it comes to mission and ministry today?

2. How are you noticing the needs, longings, and spiritual curiosity of your wider community?

3. Reflect on the characteristics of fresh expressions. What excites you? What challenges you?

4. What are ways fresh expressions of church could be vehicles for hope and healing in your community?

A FRESH EXPRESSION STORY: THE TABLE

A young adult and her husband moved to a new town with long, harsh winters. To meet people, they began to host soup nights at their home. Over soup and conversation, they begin to get to know a few other young adults, and then a few more. The evenings around their table, called "Souper Tuesdays," seemed to strike a chord with their new friends, and they clamored to continue gathering. As they continued convening around the dinner table, the hosts began to ask deeper questions—intentionally—to tap into the hopes and dreams and spiritual longings of their peers. Before long, they made a choice to explore a spiritual community outside of their home.

What started as simple soup suppers became, over time, a community of doubters and disciples committed to exploring faith together, continuing to gather around a shared meal and the Lord's Table. They called this fresh expression of faith The Table. Their small but mighty gathering began to get involved in their town, serving the marginalized and painting murals to beautify the city. A simple pot of soup and a willingness to offer hospitality became a fresh expression of church spilling God's contagious goodness into the community all around them. What could God do with a simple act of hospitality and faith in your setting?

CHAPTER TWO

THE ROOF
A Creative Way Forward

Just then some men came, carrying a paralyzed man on a bed. They were trying to bring him in and lay him before Jesus; but finding no way to bring him in because of the crowd, they went up on the roof . . .

—Luke 5:18–19

What Is Blocking the Door?

Wouldn't it be fantastic if what was blocking our twenty-first-century culture's view of Jesus was a crowded doorway to our church's worship gathering? Imagine so many people trying to press their way in that they couldn't get a glimpse of what was going on! So many of us have been deeply formed in our church communities by the prayers, the music, the teaching, and the fellowship. We long for others to find it just as meaningful!

Sadly, all the statistical data and plenty of anecdotal evidence shows a different picture. More and more inherited congregations are in full-scale decline. It's not because their doors are blocked. The "All Are Welcome" sign out front is a lovely sentiment, but it isn't often creating a stampede to our church doors.

However, what if we took seriously what actually *is* blocking the way for our twenty-first-century culture to experience a captivating encounter with Jesus? Let's consider a few:

- Negative perceptions about church
- Negative interactions with church people
- Skepticism that Christianity has anything good to offer the world
- Disconnect between the things the church is talking about and the everyday lives of people
- Distrust of institutions
- Actual judgment and harm experienced in former church experiences
- Lack of compelling interest
- Pace of life in a 24/7 culture

And that's just the tip of the iceberg.

In *The Big Sort*,[6] author Bill Bishop proposes that ever more frequently in our Western culture, particularly in the American context, people are sorting themselves into like-minded groups: Democrats sort into their Democrat bubble, Republicans sort into their Republican bubble, and, yes, Christians sort into their Christian bubble. In many cases, Christians no longer have any deep friendships or connections with anyone outside of their church.

One pastor friend of mine sent his congregation to prayerfully walk their neighborhoods during the regular worship hour one Sunday morning, with the instructions to come back for lunch to share what they had seen and learned as they looked at their neighborhoods with God's eyes and heart. One participant came back with the story: "I discovered that for years, all my neighbors have been getting together for breakfast on Sunday mornings. And I was the only one not participating. How did I get so disconnected from all the people around me?"

Frankly, by and large, those outside the church see Christians only willing to hang out with their own kind—other Christians. You know what else they see? Christians on the media fighting the culture wars, engaging in political skirmishes, outed in public scandals. Is it any wonder that so often the church door is not the entry point for people to actually encounter Jesus in a profound, life-changing way? But that changes when they get to know Dan's heart as they work side by side on environmental causes they both care about. That changes when they get to know Carolyn as she shares laughter and stories and prays with people at the laundromat. That changes when they get to experience the infectious joy of David, who is always convening block parties and volleyball games and, with a wink and a smile, announces: "Jesus loves a good party!"

What is common to all three of these situations? Proximity to a Jesus person whose life and friendship reflects good news, which begins to open up the possibility that the Jesus they follow might actually be good news.

It wasn't strangers that broke open the roof so that a man could encounter Jesus. It was friends.

What would happen if your congregation was as committed to forming friendships outside of the church walls as they are to God-honoring worship on Sunday mornings? It might just break open holes in the roof for more and more people to experience Jesus.

A Call to Creativity

For a long time, churches have labored under an attractional form of connection. We offer an amazing youth program and teenagers will flock to it. We offer a strong choir program, and musicians will not be able to resist joining in. We put on a vacation Bible school that has stunning decorations and a catchy theme and we'll draw in young families. We hire an accomplished organist or convene an amazing band, develop a relevant sermon series, and send out marketing flyers to let the community know about the amazing seasonal worship happening at First Church (Insert Your Denomination Here).

But more and more the attractional form of church isn't working. Oh, it does sometimes . . . for mostly already-Christians who are church shopping. But by and large, the events and programs of your church are lost in the cacophony of events, programs, work demands, and experiences happening in all spheres of our communities. Most people are no longer looking for more things to do.

And—for the most part—you are strangers. Can you imagine showing up on a stranger's porch and just walking into their home? That's how most people in your community feel about your church. Even if your programs are amazing and your members charming, this is your home. Not theirs. The doorway is blocked, even if you think you are inviting people in with your "All Are Welcome" sign.

So what does this mean?

We must be much more creative about how we begin to foster bridges between our congregation and the broader community.

One way the church has sought to do so is by more meaningfully engaging in the community around them and building relationships with those outside of their churches. Congregations are volunteering in local nonprofits and schools, serving the poor and marginalized in their communities, inviting neighbors to dinner, and more. This is a beautiful thing. And, at some point, these church people find the openings and the opportunities to invite those they are getting to know to join them at their church. This is also a beautiful thing. A recent survey from Lifeway revealed that one-third of people not connected with a church would go with a friend if they were invited.[7]

But here's the honest and uncomfortable truth: Many church people are embarrassed to invite people to church with them. They themselves know that the Sunday morning worship experience in their congregation probably won't resonate with their friends or the people they are coming to know—for a variety of reasons. Additionally, there are plenty of people who will brush off an invitation to join you at church—for a variety of reasons.

But what if there is another way? A way that perhaps more deeply reflects the incarnation, when Jesus came into the world and "moved into the neighborhood" (John 1:14 The Message).

What if Jesus-followers saw their natural rhythms and interests as exactly where God is animating them to serve? Delivery drivers loving and serving fellow delivery drivers. Golfers pouring into their golf group. Runners training together. Neighbors gathering their neighbors. Food pantry volunteers eating with food pantry clients.

What if Jesus-followers stayed in these relationships, thoughtfully loving and mutually serving these emerging friends, and began to foster a deepening spiritual community *in the midst* of what they are already doing, where people already are? Not forcing conversions or pushing church on people, but rather doing life with people in ways that naturally foster and follow people's curiosity toward Jesus and a community that reflects the shalom of Jesus.

During the pandemic, one of our baristas was an out-of-work actor. With all theaters closed for the foreseeable future, he took to making coffee. It wasn't his dream job. But it paid the bills. Over time, he got to know some Christians, not by coming to Sunday worship services, but through over-the-counter banter, encouragement, and taking interest in the things that interested him. Over time, as relationships with this young actor grew, a church leader asked him to consider sharing his love for acting by performing a dramatic retelling of the Pentecost story for our congregation. He agreed. Let me tell you, when he told the story of Pentecost through the eyes of someone new to the story, you could have heard a pin drop. Some weeks later, the church leader proposed another idea: "Would you be open to developing a one-act play based on the Gospel of Mark? You develop it. You perform it. And all the proceeds of any ticket sales go to you." So this "I'm-not-really-into-the-church-thing" barista immersed himself in the Gospel of Mark. The night of the performance, the room was filled with a mixture of college theater friends, coffee shop patrons, and church people . . . and the performance was stunningly brilliant. At the end of the evening, with tears in his eyes, the young man received a bear hug from his father who told him, "I've never been more proud of you." The kingdom of God was visceral in that room. And unfolding in the lives of those who would probably never go church shopping. Most importantly, the starting point of that journey wasn't a church-led program or a marketing brochure; it was a willingness to delve into the hopes and longings of a young actor . . . and point him to the possibility of exploring Jesus.

What might it look like to form ongoing spiritual community among actors and improv enthusiasts? If Sunday morning worship services and men's retreats don't energize the aspiring actors in your community, then what could?

It seems no accident that at the same time church choirs are on the decline, pop-up pub choirs are standing room only. We were made to worship! How can we open up opportunities for people to connect that heartbeat with the God who loves them?

How amazing would it be to see forms of church that made the gospel come alive for artists and addicts and adrenaline junkies and more . . . and perhaps even reanimated bored Christians who are discovering that giving yourself away for the sake of others is actually the way to life that truly is life. Or as Paul prayed for the Ephesians: "I pray that you may have the power to comprehend, with all the saints, what is the breadth and length and height and depth, and to know the love of Christ that surpasses knowledge, so that you may be filled with all the fullness of God" (3:18–19).

An Invitation into Diversity

Did you notice in this Scripture passage that there was a doorway *and* a hole in the roof?

Fresh expressions are not about discarding all the amazing things about your existing church, what we often call the "inherited church" in this movement. The congregations we see today have emerged from the deep and rich inheritance of those who have come before us. Those traditions, communities of care, liturgies; those histories of deep wrestling with theology and the mystery of Christ; those hours upon hours of serving the poor and the hurting; those soaring cathedrals and lovingly crafted sanctuaries—this is not a call for all of that to be discarded. You are probably in this conversation, reading this book, because you came to know Christ and what it means to follow Christ in community through a local church. People can and will still encounter the grace and transformation of Christ in these spiritual communities.

But simply put, those existing forms of church will increasingly not connect with a growing number of people in our postmodern twenty-first-century culture. No amount of contemporary worship bands and institutional reorganization strategies are likely to move the needle on that front.

Fresh expressions are about new forms of church coming alongside (not replacing) inherited congregations. In the way of the Good Shepherd, who leaves the ninety-nine to go out and find the lost and the left out (Luke 15:3–7), the church begins to take seriously those who their existing church cannot reach and innovates new forms of community that can more naturally connect in a changing world. Following the one who sent the disciples into the towns and villages (Luke 10:1), the existing church sends the everyday people in their pews to inhabit the places and spaces and relationships of their everyday lives in the way of Jesus. Some of those seeds take root and form new, (typically) micro-communities where faith is explored, formed, and lived out . . . right in the places that they took root. These new shoots don't take over the landscape, they grow up *alongside* the existing congregation.

Or to repeat the Scripture analogy, this is about church doors *and* roof holes.

What does this look like practically?

It looks like one small congregation that has a traditional Sunday morning gathering. The men's group and women's groups meet for Bible study during the week. A small cadre of volunteers teaches Sunday school with the children. The flower guild arranges flowers and the choir sings in worship. A little food pantry cabinet sits at the entry to the parking lot, and the congregation is involved in a couple of local serving initiatives in their community.

- *And* a couple of church members have begun to gather a group of widows for lunch and conversation.
- *And* a couple of retired teachers have begun to tutor four children and gather their families for a potluck dinner together every other week.
- *And* a group of three families concerned about food insecurity around the neighborhood of the church gathers neighbors once a month for breakfast on the grounds next to the food pantry cabinet.

In our setting, it looks like a regular . . . maybe even quirky . . . Sunday morning congregation with an English-speaking worship service and Spanish-speaking worship service. There is an active youth group, a Sunday school program for children, a large children's camp each summer, small groups, and plenty of mission opportunities.

- *And* a weekly fresh expression with day laborers (who for countless reasons will not join our Sunday morning congregation *even though we have a service in Spanish*).
- *And* a Messy Church, a group of adults and children pursuing faith together through creativity and active exploration led by a local mom with neighbors and friends.
- *And* a cul-de-sac fresh expression that emerged in a neighborhood during the pandemic.

- *And* a coffee shop that provides a natural space for connection points between the church and the community.
- *And* Front Porch Community Dinners that gather monthly in the coffee shop to share a meal and hear one another's stories.

Each of these fresh expressions offers a unique opening for people who are not walking in our sanctuary doors on a Sunday morning. And through both the inherited church *and* these fresh expressions on the edges, a more diverse group of people are better able to experience the life of the gospel.

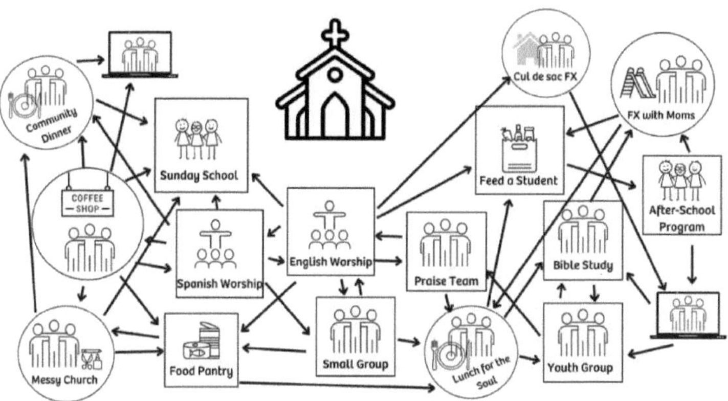

In this way, a flourishing ecosystem has the opportunity to take root, where existing churches and a vast array of micro-communities offer different openings for people to encounter the transforming love of Jesus and life in meaningful Christian community.

A Vision for a Blended Ecology

I live in suburban Washington, DC. Minutes from my home may be snarled traffic and high-stakes politics, but out my back window, you may be surprised to discover that there is an alternate reality. It's an ecosystem teeming with a wholly different kind of life. Here, deeply rooted mature trees coexist with emerging new saplings, creating homes for all kinds of creatures from birds and insects to foxes and deer. Here, a stream sustains life for flora and fauna. Here, different forms of life depend on one another for the whole ecosystem to thrive. Here, children play and dig and build and explore, freed from the relentless cultural pressure to perform and succeed. Here, adults enjoy the wonder of creation, walk their dogs, and exhale from the frenetic pace of life.

In the fresh expression context, we are discovering that what starts as a congregation willing to plant seeds of new Christian community can over time become a flourishing *blended ecology* ecosystem. The deep-rooted tree, a metaphor of the inherited church, is no longer just standing alone in a plot of dirt baking in the sun and trying to survive. Now she finds herself among emerging forms of church—which bring new life into the ecosystem—changing the whole environment as vibrant life cascades throughout the system. Now, like the metaphor of the ecosystem out my back door, there is play and exploration and digging and exhaling as a diversity of people are beginning to discover this place of life pulsing with the fullness of Jesus.

Inherited churches need fresh expressions. Through fresh expression experimentation, the inherited church gets a front-row seat to real-time learning about impactful ministry in the twenty-first century. In her connection with fresh expression initiatives, the inherited church often sees her own passion for mission and evangelism reanimated, a posture that is directly correlated with increased vitality. The inherited church also begins to see members growing in discipleship as they lead these fresh expressions and bear the fruit of new disciples.

In the same way, fresh expressions benefit from the inherited church. It's the inherited church, her care and mentoring and deep theology and traditions, that forms the pioneering leaders of these missions. The inherited church has people and financial resources that can be shared for the sake of God's kingdom. Fresh Expression leaders can benefit from the ongoing mentoring of inherited church leaders. And, sometimes, new disciples who are maturing in their faith in a fresh expression context will even find themselves curious enough to dip their toe into the inherited church that was willing to radically love them enough to give them a spiritual community that could feel like home.

Together, fresh expressions and inherited churches can not only coexist, but actually bless one another. And, arm in arm, they allow ever more people to discover vibrant life in God's kingdom.

The Impact of a Blended Ecology Approach

Think about your investment portfolio. Does your financial advisor suggest that you put all your savings into one investment, or do they recommend a diversified investment strategy? Of course, the answer is a diversified strategy. That way, if one investment doesn't do well, other investments can balance that out. A diversified strategy doesn't guarantee your financial future but does increase the likelihood.

For a long time, the Western church has dabbled in only one modality of church. As the church adds a few fresh expressions to the mix, it begins to diversify the portfolio. Most importantly, this diversity increases the faithful witness of Christ's church. Diverse peoples engaged with the gospel in meaningful ways has the potential to add beautiful dimensions to the body of Christ. Churches connecting with people through multiple expressions are better oriented to step into a future of accelerating change. Best of all, churches with this diverse approach get a front-row seat to the expanding kingdom of God here on earth!

More people engaging in life with Jesus . . . more *different kinds* of people engaging in life with Jesus . . . and a stronger possibility that your church will not only survive but thrive in a changing world: the diversified approach just makes sense!

Forget the Financial Advisor . . . What Does Scripture Show Us?

The Jerusalem Church in Acts hit a decision point. Was there going to be a requirement as the mission went out for every emerging community to conform to particularities of the inherited church? Was there going to be only one approach for communities of Christ-followers?

Or was there room for particularity in different contexts? After some controversy . . . and, of course, quite a few church meetings . . . it was decided that there were some essentials to hold onto, but outside of that, this profoundly beautiful guidance: "It seemed good to the Holy Spirit and to us not to burden you with anything beyond those requirements" (Acts 15:28 NIV).

It seemed good to the Holy Spirit. And to us. That the mission not be constrained unnecessarily. The church in Antioch didn't have to be an exact replica of the church of Jerusalem. The stability and depth of Jerusalem had value. The forming community in Antioch, those who were hearing about Jesus for the first time, might look different, but it had great value too. The Jerusalem church, the consummate inherited church, was led by the Holy Spirit to diversify the mission for the sake of the gospel.

From there, they blessed and encouraged Paul to continue in his mission. The Jerusalem church continued her ministry with the traditions and practices that animated the primarily Jewish congregation, and at the same time, they sent out Paul and others to ripple out the witness among the Jews and Gentiles in all kinds of different spaces and places. The essential witness remained the same—Jesus is Lord!—yet the practices around community and God-honoring lives began to take different shapes and forms.

We see in Acts 16 the Holy Spirit animating this mission—guiding, directing, redirecting, bringing specific people and places to mind, and infusing the mission with a bold witness. The missionaries see a vision of a man from Macedonia, but surprisingly, the Holy

Spirit leads them to a place of prayer by the river, where they meet, not a man, but Lydia in the marketplace of her purple cloth business. There, the Lord opens the hearts of many, and Lydia's entire household is baptized. They begin meeting regularly in her home, and a fresh expression of church is born.

Over and over, Paul's mission takes him to the synagogue *and* the marketplace, places where religious people already gathered *and* where the Spirit was doing a new thing. This is the blueprint for the mission of the church: "But you will receive power when the Holy Spirit comes on you; and you will be my witnesses in Jerusalem, and in all Judea and Samaria, and to the ends of the earth" (Acts 1:8 NIV).

God has poured out the Holy Spirit on Christ's church. That we may be witnesses in all the spaces and places of this world so loved by God.

Sometimes the witness beckons people to doorways. And sometimes, the witness invites Christ-followers to make holes in the roof.

This Takes a Bit of Courage

I have a hunch it took a bit of courage to make a hole in someone's roof. After all, what will the neighbors think? What if it doesn't work? What if we accidentally fall through? What about the monetary damage incurred? How much will that repair cost?

Because starting a fresh expression means going a little off-script from the usual forms of ministry, the idea can often feel a bit daunting. There are always risks in trying new things in new places, and you may wonder if a bit of doubt and fear makes you somehow ill-equipped to do this work. You may be concerned about naysayers in your congregation that will be skeptical about this approach to ministry, and when you imagine the push-back you might receive, it gives you pause.

And yet, the bigger question is: What is the risk if we don't do it?

It's okay if every seed planted doesn't take root. But some will. So take the risk. Pray for courage. Because we need doors and holes—inherited churches and fresh expressions of church—if we are going to point an anxious, disconnected, skeptical, struggling, dehuman-ized, lonely postmodern world to the Great Healer.

Discussion Questions

1. What do you think might be blocking the door for people in the community around you to encounter Jesus?

2. How does the vision of a blended ecology in your local congregation excite you? How does it challenge you?

3. What ideas are beginning to come to mind as you think about your church expressing itself in more than one form?

4. What's the risk if your congregation does not begin to make this shift?

A FRESH EXPRESSION STORY: WHO LET THE DADS OUT

A new dad was looking to connect with other dads in the community for friendship and support during a new season of life. There was a men's small group at the church, but it was mostly guys who had been together for a long time. Moreover, this dad did not want to leave his child to go meet with other men after working long hours all week, nor did he want to saddle his wife with more solo parenting time while he went out with the guys. He wondered if there were other dads who wanted to spend time with their child in a social environment while forming friendships with other dads.

He began to choose locations to meet up with other dads once a month—a coffee shop, the playground, a splash pad, a nature trail—and he got the word out through the daycare and neighborhood community. Before long, dads were becoming friends, chatting together about the joys and challenges of parenting, sharing prayers for one another, and exploring how being an earthly father was helping them to discover the unconditional love of a heavenly Father. In a season that can feel disorienting and isolating, these dads are discovering the power of encouraging, playful community that is helping them explore life, faith, and parenting together. Who Let the Dads Out is fun for dads, fun for kids, and fun for moms who get a morning free from responsibilities! It is a simple, no-cost Fresh Expression that any dad in your congregation can do.

CHAPTER THREE

THE JOURNEY TO JESUS
How Fresh Expressions Form

They were trying to bring him in and lay him before Jesus; but finding no way to bring him in because of the crowd, they went up on the roof and let him down with his bed through the tiles into the middle of the crowd in front of Jesus.

—LUKE 5:18B–19

An Incremental Journey

I wasn't prepared for the abrupt descent. I was flying into Tegucigalpa, Honduras, and was not familiar with the topography. We banked one way, then the other, and then—*whoosh*—a startling drop. It was at that moment that I noticed almost all the Hondurans on the plane praying, clutching their rosaries. . . . They knew what I had failed to anticipate. The journey was a bit precarious and needed an attentive pilot. There came a solid thud and the squeal of brakes. Then the spontaneous outbreak of applause. We had arrived.

The paralyzed man did not arrive in front of Jesus because he was unceremoniously dropped with a thud from the rafters. He was thoughtfully, attentively, and, thankfully, incrementally lowered by friends. We'll take a look at the friends in the next chapter, but for now, let's focus on the journey to Jesus.

Though there was an idea at the outset—"We should try the roof!"—we sometimes miss the reality that to get their friend to Jesus required some time, energy, and effort. It began from a place of compassion, but it was a process, not an instant result. Likewise, when love stirs us to journey with people toward Jesus, it takes some care and intentionality.

On the one hand, we don't want to do damage in our fervor to introduce people to Jesus. But, on the other hand, we don't want to neglect the opportunity for people to actually encounter Jesus. How do we do this? Through what Fresh Expressions often calls a loving-first journey.

We begin to embody the life and nature of Jesus in a journey *with* people, rather than thinking up a program *for* people. We help them experience love and belonging in a healing community that reflects the passionate love of Jesus for the world. And we help people discover the love and compassion of Jesus right where they are, inviting them into the grace-infused life.

In the Scripture passage, they lowered the man to Jesus on *his mat*, allowing the familiar to intersect with the holy. In a nutshell, that's the way of fresh expressions.

The Loving-First Journey

Think about a time when you felt like you mattered, like you were seen, like you were loved.

Now, think about a time when you were treated like a marketing target. Or, perhaps, like someone's project. Feel the difference?

Our culture is awash with marketing techniques, meant to serve the interests of the organization. Fresh expressions are not another church-growth scheme or marketing strategy.

Instead, if you sense God inviting you to go on this Fresh Expression journey, it is important to set out with the intention to love people with the compassion of Jesus. Here's the real question: If this person *never* takes seriously the Jesus thing, never quite steps fully into your dream for what a new Christian community could be, would you still love them? I mean, boots-on-the-ground, show-up, never-give-up kind of love. The world is watching. Are we only interested in making the sale or are we about deeply loving people with the unconditional love of Jesus?

The Fresh Expression journey is, at its core, a loving-first journey, because as Paul's letter to the church in Corinth reminds us, without love we are noisy gongs and clanging cymbals (1 Cor. 13:1). As we begin to unpack the Fresh Expression journey, you may notice that it doesn't start with a program or a logo or a three-year strategy. It starts with a priority of love.

So if you are ready to step into this posture of loving people, no strings attached, then read on and let's get practical about what this journey can look like.

How Do Fresh Expressions Start?

The Fresh Expression journey is not a recipe to follow step by step until... *voilà*—you have a successful outcome. Think of it more like learning the principles of cooking. If you learn the principles of salt, fat, acid, and heat, for instance, you can apply those principles no matter what you are cooking. In the same way, the Fresh Expressions journey is a set of principles that can be applied in any setting, any size community, any context, any language.

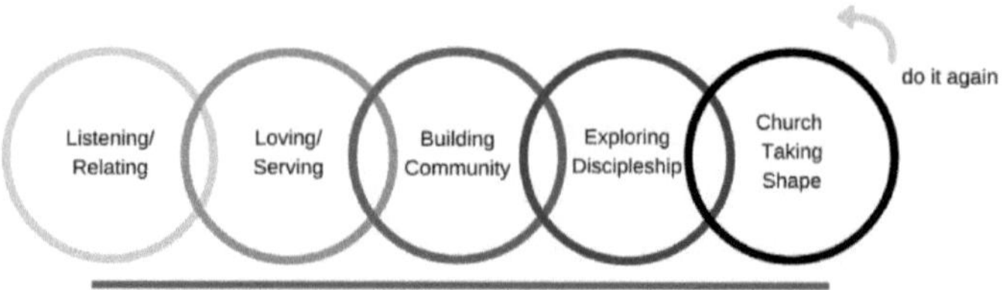

A fresh expression of church often starts with an agenda no more complicated than a disciple of Jesus (or a group of disciples) being willing to immerse time and energy into loving and listening. Listening and loving helps them discover ways to build community and explore discipleship. Over time, this community becomes a place where the good news of Jesus can be experienced, and also a place where it can be tested and practiced in community. As rhythms of spiritual practices, care for one another, forgiveness and restoration, side-by-side servanthood, and forms of communal worship begin to unfold, a contextual church starts to take shape. Some whose faith has deepened through this community will sense the invitation to share this kind of life with another community of people, doing again what they have instinctively learned is the life of faith . . . disciples who disciple others.

That is a very simple description of what pastor and author Eugene Peterson often calls "a long obedience in the same direction."[8] In other words, this journey can't be hurried. It takes time. It takes humility. But it also takes intentionality. So let's break down some of the principles along this journey.

How Do Fresh Expressions Emerge?

Typically, fresh expressions prayerfully emerge around people, places, or passions.

- *People groups:* This could be people in a particular season of life (young parents, active adults, single moms), or people who share a common interest (running or knitting or role-playing games), or anything else that people may have in common. Our culture is replete with different subcultures that may serve as starting points for fresh expressions mission.
- *Place:* This could be a neighborhood, an apartment complex, an assisted living unit, a workplace, or a local brewery or café. These create geographic connections

and natural hang-out spaces that can be the starting point for fresh expressions mission.

- *Passions:* Fresh expressions can form around shared passions, such as environmental concerns, justice issues, food insecurity, socio-economic disparity, refugee support, foster children, and more. This shared heartbeat is a natural connecting point to develop community as you work together to do something good in the world.

Notice that these are starting places, not ending points. Fresh expressions start with a people that God is calling you to befriend (or deepen existing friendships) and build community. The clearer you are about the *who* of the mission, the more contextual you can be in the mission. You are not seeking to develop exclusive enclaves of like-minded people. Yet, new Christian communities are most likely to take root where there are ways people can—and perhaps already are—naturally connecting. At the same time, know that a shared journey of faith will most certainly lead to boundary crossing relationships, and the Holy Spirit may send us in a direction we didn't anticipate or to people we didn't anticipate. One leader set out to start a new community in a geographical neighborhood and wound up with a community of mostly international students. Start with those that God places in your path or on your heart, but don't be surprised by what else may unfold!

Regardless of whether you are sensing a call to a people, place, or shared passion, there are some common principles and practices that lead to fresh expressions of church.

Listening

Listening is actively paying attention on several fronts: to a specific community, to our own interest/passions/networks, and to God.

Our first act of listening is to God. Through spiritual disciplines such as prayer, Bible study, and conversations with other disciples, we may begin to get glimpses of how God is already at work. We may recognize God breaking our hearts for a particular people or giving us new eyes to see our friendships or our community. We may notice God opening some doors or closing some doors of opportunity. We may sense God inviting us to have conversations with specific people. As we listen and are open to God's leading, God sometimes gives us a clear vision of what a healing presence could look like in a particular context. Other times, the details are hazier to us, yet we sense the nudging of the Spirit to take some steps of faith even as we continue to seek discernment of God's will.

At the same time, we are listening in a specific community with whom God is asking us to be present. That may be the neighborhood right around your church—or a specific neighborhood that God is bringing to mind. It may also be a particular subculture or network. Our North American culture is filled with myriad networks that share interests (gaming, knitting, pickleball), work (tech or health care or farming), passions (support for victims of human trafficking, tutoring, mental health support), stages of life (caregivers, single young adults, preschool families), and more.

Saint Francis of Assisi once prayed, "O Divine Master, Grant that I may not so much seek . . . to be understood as to understand."[9] You aren't going into the community to tell people how great your church is; you are trying to deeply listen so that you can better understand—so you can begin to hear their stories, their longings, their hopes and dreams. Asking questions of influencers, teachers, community leaders, and business owners can give you some clues to the hopes and hurts of a community.

However, don't neglect the casual conversations with everyday people that are invaluable to the listening process. Spend some time in third places. What are third places? They are natural places where people in the community spend time. This term was popularized by sociologist Ray Oldenberg and refers to spaces in a person's life where they spend the most time apart from work and home. These spaces are accessible, playful, neutral spaces where regulars and newcomers alike are welcomed and received with ease.[10] So go hang out in third places and see what you learn just by participating. Play trivia at Trivia Night. Strike up a conversation with your server at the café. Ask curious questions of the librarian. Spend time at the County Fair. Just as Jesus traveled among all the cities and villages (Matt. 9:35), spend some time paying attention in yours.

Extensive demographic data is often available—and you will want to explore that information—but it can't take the place of the stories of people. It is through the process of listening to people and their stories that we disrupt our tendency to make assumptions about what people need or want and discover what might actually resonate with our neighbors.

We also need to pay attention to how we are wired.

- What interests do we have?
- What skills do we have?
- What in the world breaks our hearts?
- What animates us to action?
- Where are our social networks and who do we already know?

Sometimes these are clues to ways we have natural intersections with others whom God might want to engage for this mission. One leader worked at a running store and knew all the avid runners in town, which created a natural open door for him to start a fresh expression along the local running trail. Another leader knew Spanish, her heart broke for new immigrant families in her small community, and she had a local library card. As she listened to God and to her community, she wound up in a conversation with the local librarian. That opened the door to a summer Spanish book reading program with children. Through that opportunity, she got to know their mothers. Over time, as she listened, she began to better understand how she could love and serve these families—which brings us to our next principle.

Loving People

We don't start with a new worship service, we start with loving people through friendship and acts of service. This is not about fixing people or solving problems; this is about being an agent of contagious goodness in the lives of people. That act of service may be as simple as sharing a meal, jumping their dead battery, or helping them move. Or it could mean meeting physical needs that we are becoming more aware of as we listen.

In the process of loving and serving, we invest ourselves in forming new friendships or deepening existing friendships with people outside of the church. Remember, we are not in this journey targeting people for conversion; we are on a journey with people into mutual friendship, with the prayer that in God's time they might experience the joy of friendship with God as well.

Building Community

As we build friendships with our neighbors and foster or deepen connections among a group of people, a sense of community often emerges. What began as casual conversations or shared activities begins to bond a group into a deeper sense of connection. This is a clue that a community is beginning to take shape. Social gatherings may start to emerge around shared interests, often meeting in homes or cafés or community spaces. Fresh expressions have emerged from group hikes, community garden chores, food pantry set-up, and more. You'll know that community is being experienced when you hear things that reflect a sense of belonging like, "*We* are always here on Wednesdays" or a sense of collective connection, such as "Remember that time when *we* got lost on the trail?"

What do the first gatherings look like? There is no one way to do this. You will take your cues from the level of relationship you have and the good listening you have already done. Some gatherings start right away with prayer, spiritual conversation, or a well-told Jesus story. Others will trend more toward a social environment that is attentive to fostering deeper connection and friendship and build toward spiritual conversation over time. It is, however, important to winsomely out yourself as a Jesus-follower from the outset, so consider how to do so in ways that are authentic to you and would best fit the context. Release your need to follow a rigid agenda, be fully present with people, and follow the nudgings of the Holy Spirit.

Exploring Discipleship

Though making disciples may be the heart of the mission, a fresh expression doesn't manipulate or force people into faith. We go on a journey with people in the direction of Jesus, being attentive to the way that the Holy Spirit is at work in people and the life of the community. That can take place in informal and more formal ways.

Informal discipleship occurs in the midst of everyday life, among ever deepening friendships. In the context of community, people may begin noticing that there is a way that we value and relate with each other or with our town that provokes curiosity, and maybe they begin to ask some questions about that. In my setting, that looked like a single mom who made this observation: "I didn't know family could feel like this." Observations like these are ripe opportunities for exploration. Conversations about spiritual issues may naturally arise out of the friendships that we are living out with people. As people grapple with their lives and regrets and longings, we may find ourselves invited into profound opportunities to explore the possibility of a God who loves them. Mentoring, intentional conversations, and curious questions are the way that Jesus shaped his disciples . . . perhaps it gives us a roadmap to how we can be faithful in our settings today. As followers of Jesus live authentic lives in close proximity with people, discipleship happens.

Formal discipleship occurs through organized opportunities that allow people to learn about the way of Jesus, such as prayer groups, discussion groups, Jesus stories, Bible explorations, or acts of compassion and mercy. Don't let the word "formal" throw you if preaching and presentation is the way you've typically been discipled—in a fresh expression the learning is often much more dialogue and discovery oriented. These are always opt-in opportunities, never forced group activities or hidden agendas. They don't take the place of the community gatherings that are already taking place; they emerge alongside them. Sometimes you notice that a few are spiritually curious, and you invite this small group of folks to join you another night of the week to wrestle with their questions. Perhaps you let people know that you will be available to pray with anyone who is interested after the group gathering. Sometimes, it's thoughtfully offering opportunities for the group to give voice to a collective sense of grief following a local tragedy. With time, you may notice that there is interest in more robustly exploring Scripture and Christian life together, and that's a clue that God is up to something.

Often, Scripture exploration takes the form of simple questions that everyone can engage, no matter how far along they are in their journey of faith. Questions like:

- If the story happened today, what would it look like?
- What is this story showing or telling me?
- If this were true, how could it make a difference in my life?

To be sure, the exploring discipleship part of the journey is one of the hardest aspects of the fresh expression journey to imagine. I mean, how do you move from being a social group to a discipling community? Isn't this awkward at best or manipulative at worst? Let's unpack this a little bit more. There are two ways that fresh expressions of church tend to emerge:

1. From the start
2. Organically developing over time and relationship

What is best for a particular mission always depends on the group and the context. Some fresh expressions start at the outset as a curiously different form of church, so people already have some inkling that this will have a faith component to it. For example, "Adventure Church" or "Farm Church." This may make sense in contexts where people are not interested in traditional church but would be intrigued by compelling alternative experiences.

However, in some contexts, especially increasingly post-Christian ones, starting with church will create an automatic barrier. In this scenario, discipleship will only emerge after a long investment of friendship and community gatherings and will often emerge among a subset of the larger group. These individuals begin to show signs of interest in faith exploration, and an attentive leader will begin to foster opt-in opportunities for those in the group who are interested in these kinds of conversations and practices. Sometimes, the whole group is ready to be invited into something deeper, but more often it is particular individuals within the larger group who are beginning to exhibit openness. In either case, the form of church that will emerge will be shaped by the culture where people are coming alive in the faith. For example, regular neighborhood community gatherings led a leader to offer bonfire nights for some who had expressed interest in wanting to engage more deeply around the big life questions of young adulthood. Bonfire nights became an opt-in gathering for honest sharing of their deep questions, fears, and insecurities, which became a place to grapple with the possibility of a God who loved them. By engaging discipleship among the subset of the larger group over s'mores, a holy community began to form as these raw conversations led them to the feet of Jesus.

Church Taking Shape

As disciples are beginning to form, a Jesus-centered community may begin to emerge. New disciples are finding that it is life-giving to associate with others on the same journey. Those who are coming to faith help to shape the rhythms of the community that will foster their spiritual growth. The leader begins to thoughtfully incorporate some of the treasures of this ancient faith, such as worship and sacraments, in ways that fit naturally in the new context. It is important to not just default to styles and patterns that are comfortable for traditional church settings, but rather consider how these ancient practices can find meaning among the new group that is coming to faith. In one setting, a Scripture passage is read before a group paddle. There is an ease to the banter amidst the beauty of the river with each stroke of the paddles. At the end of the paddle, the group shares the insights that emerged from encountering the story around a shared meal, concluding their time together with the Lord's Supper and the commitment to live out self-giving love in one tangible way the following week. Word, worship, prayer, table, fellowship, offering, acts of mercy . . . sounds a lot like some of the enduring marks of church to me.

How will you know this fresh expression initiative is maturing as a form of church? You will see growing evidence of four dimensions of relationship developing: Up/In/Out/Of.

The community is growing in its worship and communion with the trinitarian God (Up). There are maturing practices of caring deeply for one another and commitment to mutual lives of fellowship (In). They evidence a care and concern for the world that beckons them to follow Christ into mission, mercy, and justice with others (Out). And they are beginning to understand that, though a unique flavor of Christian community in a particular context, they are part of the wider body of Christ, baptized into the church universal (Of).

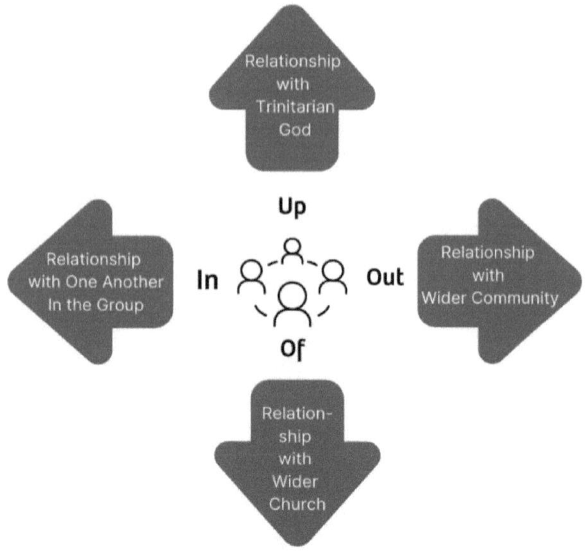

Do It Again

Each disciple has friends, networks, and interests. Because they have been shaped in a community in which everyone participates in sharing faith and community life—rather than being passive recipients—they begin to see they, too, can start a fresh expression of church with a new group of people. People who have been brought into spiritual community through this journey will not know another way—it will be a natural outgrowth of the faith they have received.

Undergirded by Prayer

This is not a work of merely human effort. Fresh expressions of church are a work of the Holy Spirit. Throughout the journey, commitment to prayer and discernment will help you follow the promptings of the Holy Spirit. We can't control the outcomes; only God can open hearts and transform lives.

This is a movement soaked in prayer. Pray that God will send out co-laborers for the harvest. Pray to have eyes to see the people among whom God wants to send you. Pray to meet people who will resonate with the vision, and pray for persons of peace who will not only be excited about the vision, but will open doors, broker connections, and provide an ongoing presence that builds local trust in you and this mission. Pray for discernment for the next right step, and pray that God would manifest the fruit of the Spirit in you as you go. Don't be shocked that God may surprise you all along the way with situations or people that you could not have imagined or written into the script of your Fresh Expression journey.

Patience and Perseverance

On paper, the framework looks rather neat and tidy, as if one thing leads to the next and to the next, in an orderly fashion. In practice, it's messier. If you've ever been a new parent reading all the parenting books, you discovered that though you could apply the principles, you couldn't control the process. Children grow and go through stages that you can't control. One day, you think you've got this parenting thing down, the next day you wonder if you are really equipped for this. You may find the same kinds of emotions welling up as you lead a fresh expression mission. You can't control the pacing of building a sense of deep community, just as you can't predetermine when a subset of the group will be ready for formal discipleship. Relationships take time, and spiritual curiosity can't be rushed.

You may start something like a dinner church, in which Jesus stories are part of the shared community meal from the onset, but you realize you don't yet have a trusting community where informal discipling can take hold, so you have to loop back to listening for ways God is inviting you to love and build deeper bonds of friendship and community. On the other hand, you may start a pottery class with the hopes that down the road artistic expression could be the onramp to discovering a creative God, but the second class, someone begins sharing about a recent loss and you recognize that the group has suddenly moved from playful creativity to solidarity in loss, and you have crossed a spiritual threshold long before you ever expected. In addition, every situation is different; some leaders are starting this journey with robust community connections and well-formed friendships and others are starting this mission from the ground up.

The patience and perseverance of the friends in our Scripture passage can be instructive as we set out on this journey with people. Because it mattered to them that their friend had an opportunity to encounter Jesus, they didn't give up. Investing in people is not always comfortable or easy. There are always risks involved. You may face failures and heartbreak along the way. But take heart, because the opportunity to be a part of lives getting a taste of the gospel through Christian community is a treasure that will change your life too.

Discussion Questions

1. Notice that this is a loving-first journey, not a program-first journey. What about this shifts your framework for mission and outreach?

2. How have you already been listening in your community? How might you engage in more listening after exploring the Fresh Expression journey in this chapter?

3. Is there a people, place, or passion that has come to mind for you as you think about the possibility of fresh expressions in your setting?

4. What is God revealing to you as you pay attention to the Spirit's leading?

A FRESH EXPRESSION STORY: LUNCH FOR THE SOUL

In a local community, the immigration debate became a national flashpoint. A media frenzy ensued and day laborers became a political debate. Yet Edwin saw a group of scared, hungry young men. He knew something about being new to a country. He knew something about being hungry. So he went and sat down on the street corner with these men, bags of sandwiches in hand. He got to know them, heard their stories, lamented with them, and he came back to be with them again. And again. As these day laborers began to experience his friendship and trust him, he found ways to pray with them and invite them into exploring the Bible together. The media left. But Edwin kept coming back. In time, Edwin reached out to a nearby local church and inquired about partnering to provide a hot meal and a safe gathering space. This congregation became a willing, enthusiastic partner, and Lunch for the Soul went from curbside conversation to a large noonday meal for all who didn't get work that day. The meal is robust, but the conversation, encouragement, and worship are even more so.

In this fresh expression of church, scared and struggling day laborers find connection with a God who loves them and a community that cares for them even when day-to-day life can be precarious. And in the beautiful unfolding of the church of Jesus Christ, some of these men, being shaped by their growing faith, have become everyday missionaries themselves, going on a mission trip to renovate the gathering space of another emerging expression of church. From recipient of God's grace to ambassadors of God's grace. This is how God is at work in fresh expressions.

CHAPTER FOUR

THE FRIENDS

Who Starts Fresh Expressions?

When [Jesus] saw their faith . . .

—LUKE 5:20

The Faith Enough to Take a Risk

Years ago, I heard a mother tell the story of her relationship with her daughter. Her adolescent daughter had gotten caught up in some choices and relationships that had trapped her in a spiral that was crushing her soul. Struggling with addiction, unable to extricate herself from unhealthy relationships, hollowed out, used up, and not sure what to do, she came home, utterly broken. As she wept and wept, her mother gathered her up into her lap as she had when she was a baby and rocked her, whispering in her ear, "Jesus loves you. Jesus loves you. Jesus loves you."

"I don't know if I believe that anymore," her daughter sobbed.

"That's okay, baby. I have the faith to believe it for you until you can believe it for yourself."

I've never forgotten that story.

I wonder what it would look like for congregations to have the faith and the love of this mother. Or the friends on behalf of their paralyzed friend. Would we have enough faith to draw near to people instead of waiting for people to get it together or come looking for church? Would we be willing to find the courage to make holes in roofs so that the broken and hurting and hopeless in our world could encounter the love and healing of Jesus?

Perhaps when people can experience a community of belonging, they can begin believing.

The Fresh Expression approach is an activated faith, believing enough in a God who so loved the world (John 3:16) that we would follow Jesus from our steeples into our streets, willing to invest our lives in those who have not yet gotten a real glimpse of God's kingdom or experienced God's profound love for them. Let's look at how this kind of faith response can be activated in a congregation just like yours.

Cultivating a Missional Culture

"Missional" has been a buzzword in the Western church in these last couple of decades. In a nutshell, it is an awareness that mission is not merely a function of the church, it is actually the *nature* of the church. The triune God didn't suggest our churches recruit mission committees, the triune God calls the church to join in what God is already doing in the unfolding story of redeeming the world. The

Father sent the Son, the Father and Son sent the Spirit, the Spirit sent the church. The church is sent by God into the world to be ambassadors of God's kingdom, joining God in the renewal of all things. The church is meant to be so much more than a Sunday morning worship gathering. We are sent to be a sign of love, peace, compassion, justice, and reconciliation as a witness to the risen Christ in all the everyday spaces and places of life.

Does your congregation have a mission *committee* or a mission *heart*? For many, the first step in starting a fresh expression of church will be to foster a heart for the community and world around you. I once worked with a congregation who was struggling to discern their future. Working with a small vision team, I invited them to (1) read Scripture every day, (2) intentionally walk the neighborhood as they prayed for the people, homes, businesses, and situations they noticed, (3) foster conversations with people and frequent businesses in the neighborhood around the church, and (4) pray Luke 10:2 every day (Jesus's command to pray to the Lord of the harvest for laborers to step into the abundant harvest). In their Sunday morning worship, these individuals began to share stories about the people they were meeting. They told stories about how God was already at work in the neighborhood, and they lamented gaps between God's kingdom and the present reality in the neighborhood. Simply telling these stories began to change the heart of this congregation.

What could you do to grow your congregations' heart for the neighborhood? Who is your congregation not currently engaging, and how can you shift the thinking from: *How can we get them in here?* to *How might God be asking us to go to them?* Think about how you can leverage the pulpit, board retreats, Sunday school, small groups, service projects, and more to foster a missional heartbeat in your congregation.

Another way to build a missional culture is to expand imagination of what is possible. Many people in our congregations have only known that church can exist in the form they have experienced it. What we learned from our Fresh Expressions friends in England is how important it is to tell stories about what is possible. So, tell the stories about dinner churches in trailer parks and community centers, "Faith and Friends" that explores faith in the local breweries, "Trail Church" that hikes and prays together. If you are not familiar with fresh expression stories, check out our website (www.fresh expressions.com) to connect with some of the stories that might give you a vision for the creative ways disciples are forming Christian communities in the nooks and crannies of life.

Yet another way to foster a missional culture is to fan the flames of experimentation and create an environment in which it is okay that some things will fail. Think about starting some short-term experiments: "Let's try having lemonade on the lawn after church for the next month." After a month, decide whether to keep doing it or move on to another experiment. Have you tried to host a neighborhood bonfire and no one but a few church people came? Instead of determining it was a failure, pay attention to what you can learn from the experience, and apply those learnings for the next experiment. As you try small short-term experiments in your congregation-wide ministries and outreach initiatives, you are forming your people to be more comfortable and courageous with experimentation. This behavior will begin to settle into the culture of your church and will help to unlock possibilities for fresh expression experiments.

Remember, you are forming disciples not just through your teaching but through the culture you are setting in your congregation. Are they being discipled to be primarily church attenders? Or are they being discipled to be faithful, creative, and innovative ambassadors for God in the world?

Activating the Mission Force in Your Pews: The Ministry of All Believers

You have an amazing mission force already present in your congregation. They are already in your pews. Almost every one of them has a hobby or a passion. They probably already have networks of colleagues and friends. There are places and spaces they already spend their time. Have they ever been introduced to the possibility that a fresh expression opportunity is right in front of them?

The Fresh Expressions approach does not require seminary trained leadership to form these new communities. In fact, as the Western church has become so dependent on professionalized ordained clergy, she has often lost her mission edge. Because fresh expressions are connected to a supporting inherited church, laypeople can receive the prayer, mentorship, and shaping of our theological traditions. Undergirded with this support, laypeople are fully equipped to step into the ministry of all believers, discipling others in the way of Christ through new forms of Christian community. This approach is simple, inexpensive, and effectively multiplies the opportunities for your church to connect people with the life of Jesus.

Who Starts Fresh Expressions of Church?

Every congregation has people in your pews who can help bring fresh expressions of church to life in your community. Typically, there are three ways people in your congregation can participate in helping these initiatives to emerge and thrive:

1. Pioneers
2. Permission givers
3. Supporters

Let's take a look at the value of each of these roles.

Pioneers

Pioneers are those who develop something new for the good of all.

In 1928, Alexander Fleming came home after a vacation to discover a messy lab bench and a whole lot of mold. Instead of throwing it aside, he got curious and started exploring more deeply and set off a scientific breakthrough that we now call penicillin. Fleming developed something new, something that didn't exist before.

That pioneering breakthrough was a benefit to the world, and especially those who would have died from infection, but because of penicillin, were set on a miraculous course of healing.

In the same way, Fresh Expressions Pioneers are developing new forms of church that are meant for healing of the world.

In today's world, pioneering is all about steering toward innovative ideas and leaping into new environments. We have pioneering technology advancements, pioneering research, pioneering medical breakthroughs. So, too, do we have pioneering mission leaders who steer into a love for people, a bit of creativity, and a willingness to leap into new environments.

A pioneer is simply a person of infectious hope willing to follow the Spirit into the fresh things of God.

Pioneers can be extroverts or introverts. Pioneers can be young or old or anything in between. Pioneers could be athletic or musical or neither. Pioneers can be technological wizards or technologically challenged. However, there do seem to be some common characteristics of people who are more naturally able to experiment with new forms of church.

Pioneers are often good at connecting with people, easy to relate to and to be with. They are not afraid to try new things and are often coming up with all kinds of possibilities for mission and ministry. Perhaps they've been the person on your committee who drives everyone crazy because they are always coming up with ideas that nobody else thinks the church has time or energy for.

They have a vibrant faith and they believe that life with Jesus is worth sharing with others. It's not that they never have fears or insecurities, but they are the kind of people who are still willing to take some risks, catalyze efforts, and commit time and energy for the sake of the gospel.

There may be some names that come to you right away. These are probably big "P" pioneers, those who have an infectious faith, are naturally disarming, are often entrepreneurial, and tend to easily gather community. They are wired for this kind of ministry. This is my neighbor Jim, who was frustrated serving on the facilities committee at church because what he really wanted to do was go buy an old Circuit City building and start a teen center. This is Ryan, who had served on staff at a large megachurch until he realized that what he really wanted to do was go hang out with surfers like he had done the first year of being a Christian, surfing together and talking about Jesus. This is Amanda, who just keeps gathering up the lonely and the misfits and helping them feel loved.

But you may be surprised that there are also potentially some little "p" pioneers in your midst. They may be quieter. They may not see themselves as pioneers right away. But once they catch the vision for fresh expressions, they can begin to see opportunities to connect with people groups in their everyday spheres of influence. Or they can get excited about team leading a congregation-wide fresh expression effort like a dinner church. This is the mom who gathers the other neighborhood moms together for coffee and conversation each week in her home. This is Sharlene, who was already going to the nursing home and is now discovering that she can go there not just to visit her family, but to build broader friendship and spiritual community.

Pioneers are the key leaders for your fresh expression initiatives. They step out in faith into this adventure with God, loving, serving, and gathering people in the way of Jesus.

Permission-Givers

 We had a craft box when my kids were little. My little budding artists loved to create things with the various odds and ends that were in that box. I knew that when that box came out, my kitchen was going to get a little messy. But here's the thing—their faces *lit up* when I said, "Yes, let's get down the craft box!"

There are people in our congregations who would come alive if they knew it was possible, and if they were encouraged, to experiment with a fresh expression mission. Maybe all they need is a yes and a box full of possibilities.

Permission-givers can open doors for pioneers to do their thing! They are people with influence in a church system, often pastors, elders, deacons, beloved members, or staff. If they see the value in the Fresh Expressions approach to mission, they can help to foster congregational excitement and energy around it. When a pioneer comes to them and says, "I've got this idea," they can bless and support it. When it's time to allocate resources, permission givers know how to work with the system and release financial support.

It's permission-givers who determine what gets lifted up in primary congregational gatherings like Sunday worship, and they can choose to celebrate stories of what is happening on the mission edges.

It's permission-givers who teach and preach, and they can cast a vision for what it means to be both the gathered and sent people of God.

It's permission-givers who have relational connections with congregational committees or denominational systems that can be leveraged to support the mission.

Permission-givers committed to a Fresh Expressions approach are invaluable to creating a culture that gives disciples the imagination and freedom to step into all kinds of unique new places and passions for mission.

Pastor Mike led a congregation through a sermon series exploring what it means to join God on mission today in our everyday lives. At some point in that series, he invited everyone to write down their hobbies and their community involvement on little cards and commit those to the Lord. From those cards, he set up multiple conversations with people in his congregation that he thought might be pioneers. And out of those conversations, a handful of pioneers emerged who were *lit up* about being seen and given not only permission, but encouragement, to go be on mission in motorcycle clubs, firehouses, neighborhoods, and sporting clubs. This is what permission givers can do: release pioneers into life-giving mission.

Supporters

 My kids were swimmers, and when they swam long distances, they needed support. They needed someone who could hold the counter underwater and keep them on track with their lap count, sometimes pumping the lap number underwater as if to say, "You can do it!" They needed people cheering them on as they began to get winded and lose energy. They needed coaches to urge them forward. They needed concessions workers to refuel them with snacks and Gatorade after the race.

Pioneering leaders may be the natural connectors and the key leaders for particular fresh expression initiatives. But every pioneer needs the help of supporters willing to lend a hand and cheer them on, especially because the journey takes time and intention. Supporters are those who come alongside the mission and will pray for, resource, and encourage the formation of a fresh expression. Supporters often believe deeply in the heart of the mission, even while recognizing they are not the front-line mission lead. However, they will move heaven and earth in the background to support those best suited to pioneer a new faith community. They will financially, spiritually, and practically offer what they can to help a fresh expression emerge and thrive.

A supporter's favorite question is: "What can I do to help you?" They always find ways they can help behind the scenes. They help their friends at the church understand the purpose of a fresh expression. They bake cookies, run errands, set up chairs, share events on social media, gather volunteers, and more. They give generously for the needs of the emerging community. They find ways to consistently encourage the pioneer and they pray consistently for deep community to take root. In other words, they go the extra mile to help the pioneer so that the pioneer can focus on relationships with the people.

Kristin has never started a fresh expression. But because of Kristin's commitment, a fresh expression of church with differently abled teenagers always has great snacks, a kind and patient buddy for teens needing extra support, and clean-up that is always taken care of so the pioneer can be free to spend time connecting with the families after the gathering.

Look for People of Peace

Another friend that God can sometimes provide for the mission is what we often call a "person of peace." This is not something you can script in some kind of strategic plan. But often, by God's grace, a person will emerge that is just the right person at just the right time. This is a person who resonates with what you are doing or the vision you are describing. Or, as Luke 10:6 describes, they "share in peace."

In this gospel account, Jesus sends out the disciples into what he describes as the harvest field. He invites them to go empty-handed, just themselves and the invitation to bear witness to the nearness of the kingdom of God, eating and drinking with those who welcome them. "When you enter a house, first say, 'Peace to this house.'

If someone who promotes peace is there, your peace will rest on them; if not, it will return to you" (10:5–6 NIV).

Someone who "promotes peace," as Scripture references, is not necessarily someone who is a follower of Jesus (though they can be) but someone who resonates with the peace that is being shared. They welcome you into their home or business and extend hospitality. They can open the door to their establishment and let your group meet there. They can serve as a bridge between you and the neighborhood or network you now find yourself in because they seem to know everybody! They can resource you in ways you cannot resource yourself.

How do you find people of peace? There is no formula, and you can't plan the timing of when they may come into the picture. But in God's time and God's wisdom, if you are open to the promptings of the Holy Spirit, you might see that God is sending you the partner you need for this moment in the mission.

So pray. Strike up conversations. Share your passionate vision with others. And open your eyes to the surprising, and sometimes not so surprising, people God sends your way.

It Takes a Team

The Fresh Expressions journey is not a solo effort. We were not created to live the Christian journey on our own. The same holds true for fresh expressions mission. Heroic solo leaders almost always burn out. So, it's important to find the group of people who might link up together in the efforts to start a fresh expression. They don't all need to be pioneers. Some will probably be supporters, but together they can bring a vision to life through the power of the Holy Spirit.

How many should be on the team? There's no magic number, but initial teams can be as small as two to three or as large as twelve. For example, a small fresh expression initiative in an apartment complex might need only a small team of two or three neighbors committed to listening, loving and serving, and building relationships with other neighbors. Something like a large, weekly dinner church in a local community center may require a larger team to be able to attend to the more complex requirements of a three-course meal for a large crowd.

At the same time, you don't want so many church people involved that it makes it awkward or intimidating for non-church people to connect. It may seem counterintuitive—because you *want* people from your church to be excited about a fresh expression—but remember that having a few of the right people on the bus is often more helpful than having a bus full of church people when starting a new faith community! Identify who can best help you connect with the people God is inviting you to engage. Then form a team that can help a Christian community form in that context.

Think about it this way . . . there was more than one friend on the roof with the paralyzed man, but there was not a roof full of helpers either. If there were, the roof might have caved in! Who are the people who have the faith, the heart of compassion, the shared passion, the courage to get on the roof, and the willingness to grab a rope and help? That's your team.

And don't ignore the people outside your church who God might be sending to your team! Sometimes God surprises us with teammates from other churches, or teammates who don't yet know Jesus, but somehow are animated by the vision and are open to exploring faith through service to this mission.

Discussion Questions

1. Who are some of the key permission givers in your congregation? How might their role best be leveraged to fan the flames of fresh expressions in your setting?

2. Who are some potential pioneers who come to mind after reading this chapter? What would need to happen for them to catch the vision and the possibility for fresh expressions?

3. Are there any persons of peace who God is bringing to mind?

A FRESH EXPRESSION STORY: A STOKED LIFE

Mindy and Nathan went on vacation to spend time outdoors with their family. Paddleboarding in the ocean was not only exhilarating, it revealed something that would begin to shape their hearts and imaginations. The nature lovers they were meeting in the outdoors were open-hearted about worshiping the creation, but not necessarily the Creator. Mindy and Nathan knew these were people who would never come to a traditional church, so they began to wonder, *What if we could become the bridge between nature lovers and Christian community that seeks to be God's love in the world?*

After coming home, they made a career shift and became the owners of an existing paddleboard business, which meant they had space to share their vision of a new way of connecting with people. They started convening group paddles, Paddleboard Yoga and Holy Yoga, as well as befriending all sorts of local business owners around their storefront and on the lake. Mindy and Nathan were able to start to build a community of SUP (stand up paddleboard) enthusiasts seeking community who supported one another through the difficulties of each season of life. What they found was that as one interaction became repeat interactions that became friendships, Mindy and Nathan were invited into deeper and deeper spiritual conversations with those they were coming to know.

Today, the SUP shop has become a hub for outdoor enthusiasts, robust conversation, Scripture and yoga, meet-up events and parties, community hangout space, and has expanded with the addition of a coffee shop. Nature lovers are finding faith community on the lake, nearby business owners are being blessed by and blessing this emerging community, and individuals who are coming into faith are seeking baptism.

It is possible to be a bridge to meaningful Jesus-centered community for those who are not likely to encounter Jesus in a pew, and A Stoked Life is a beautiful example of what God can do through the lives and hearts of two fellow SUP lovers who are willing to follow Jesus into a mission adventure.

CHAPTER FIVE

THE ENCOUNTER

The Impact of Fresh Expressions

When [Jesus] saw their faith, he said, "Friend, your sins are forgiven you." Then the scribes and the Pharisees began to question, "Who is this who is speaking blasphemies? Who can forgive sins but God alone?" When Jesus perceived their questionings, he answered them, "Why do you raise such questions in your hearts? Which is easier to say, 'Your sins are forgiven you,' or to say, 'Stand up and walk'? But so that you may know that the Son of Man has authority on earth to forgive sins"—he said to the one who was paralyzed—"I say to you, stand up and take your bed and go to your home." Immediately he stood up before them, took what he had been lying on, and went to his home, glorifying God. Amazement seized all of them, and they glorified God and were filled with awe, saying, "We have seen strange things today."

—LUKE 5:20–26

We Have Seen Strange Things Today!

What if we've become so comfortable in our religious practices that we are missing the opportunity to experience the joy of people coming into the life of the gospel? What if many people won't meaningfully experience the transforming power of Jesus in a worship service with three songs and a sermon? But will around a dinner table or a pickleball game or a community garden?

That's the power of fresh expressions of church.

Several years ago, I was chatting with someone who was aghast to hear about a fresh expression of church in a tattoo parlor. "Why don't you just invite those people to 'real church'?" What this person was missing is that lives are being changed right there in the tattoo parlor. Addiction and strongholds are being broken. Relationships are being restored. The literal images tattooed on human flesh that give voice to the passions and longings inside of people are being transformed into the image-bearers of Christ as they begin to discover that they are loved by God and enfolded in God's story. They gather around the risen Christ, they declare both by their worship and their tattoos that Jesus is Lord, and they share in the banquet feast at the Lord's Table. It may not look like the church you've always known, but it is the way that tattoo artists are encountering Jesus and being formed into a community centered in Christ.

The impact of fresh expressions can be profound.

Fresh Expressions Allows Jesus to Be *Experienced*

When my children were young, we went to visit family and friends who took us out on their boat. My children had never gone tubing before and when they discovered that this world of water sports existed, they wanted to try. You know what we didn't do? We didn't go back to the house and have them read an instruction manual or watch a video. Of course not! We helped them get their life jackets on, get on the tube, and experience it. First, we gave them a taste by going slow and steady, but soon, they were giving us smiles and the thumbs-up to signal they were ready for more speed.

They didn't love tubing because they heard information *about* tubing.

They loved it because it was exhilarating and they got to experience it with people who loved them!

At any given moment, anyone can google information about Christianity. The amount of online sermons, content, and devotionals is staggering. People by and large aren't looking for more information about Jesus or the church. But what if they could experience it?

Fresh expressions bring the church to people where they are in ways they can experience beloved community. Instead of receiving a glossy brochure *about* church, they can experience a group of friends loving them and exploring with them the adventure of a common life together shaped by God's grace. It is through *experience* that church becomes not that "strange, boring group that meets over there doing stuff I don't understand," but instead becomes this exhilarating community that makes life more fun, more beautiful, more purposeful, and more connected.

Instead of telling people about Jesus, we can help people experience him.

Fresh Expressions Is Making New Disciples

People who would have never come looking to join a traditional church are coming to faith in fresh expressions of church.

In a biker fresh expression, Martin was exhilarated not only to be able to go on rides with fellow Harley-Davidson owners, but to find a community that walked with him through some rocky health challenges and relationship upheaval. They showed up in his life in sacrificial ways, they spoke hope into what seemed hopeless, and gave words to the prayers he couldn't form on his own. As he discovered God's love through this community of brothers and sisters, he wanted to claim this faith as his own. And on that day that he claimed Jesus as Lord, this fellowship went wild, cheering and celebrating, and having him ring the bell, the tradition of a new Harley-Davidson owner now repurposed to display a new life purchased by God's grace.

Families are coming into the life of the gospel as they playfully explore Scripture and break bread together through Messy Church. Special-needs adults are becoming disciples as fresh expressions are being formed in workplaces where they can work and pray together. Artists are coming to faith as fresh expressions invite them to explore the Source of creativity through acts of creativity.

One day, we are going to be in the company of the saints in the presence of God, and we are going to see with our own eyes the profound ripple effects of fresh expressions. I hope on that day, you will introduce yourself to Martin . . . and so many others.

Bored Christians Are Also Coming into New Life

Darryl was planning to leave his church. He attended worship regularly, and he was part of a men's Bible study, but he was itching to do something to integrate his faith life and work life. However, every time he approached church leaders about serving more intentionally, they wanted to plug him into a church committee. No one was encouraging him to think outside the system, so Darryl felt like he had to leave the system.

But what if Darryl were given a vision for fresh expressions? What if he didn't leave the church but rather embraced the Fresh Expression journey amidst the business he envisioned starting?

There are bored Christians in many of our churches. One pastor tells the story of a parishioner who went through all the versions of discipleship classes. At the conclusion of the last one, this faithful church member looks at his pastor and says, "Is this all there is?"

There are countless church members who would come alive in a fresh expression setting. They have a heart for people who don't know God's love, things they love to do, and they would be invigorated to discover that God could be inviting them to start something new doing what they love with others and with God.

One dinner church leader looked around at all the laughter and hugs around the tables, and tearfully shared with her team, "I can't believe I finally get to be a part of something that my grandchildren want to be a part of."

Fresh expressions don't just change the lives of participants, they also reanimate the lives of those who lead them.

Raising the Spiritual Temperature

One of the most commonly asked questions at Fresh Expressions training is this: Will these efforts grow *our church*? The undercurrent of this question is always whether this approach will get more people to sit in our pews on Sunday morning. Not necessarily. However, here is what does happen over time. As bored Christians become animated, as new disciples are being made and these stories are being shared with the existing congregation, over time, the evangelism energy and spiritual vitality of the congregation grows. Even for those who are not directly relating to the fresh expression.

The way your congregation prays for the community may begin to change.

The way your congregation understands the parables of the lost sheep and the prodigal son may begin to change.

The way your congregation trusts that God is actively at work in the world may begin to change.

This opening up begins to increase the spiritual temperature of your congregation. One congregation had been just going through the motions for a long time. Membership had dwindled and they wondered if they could even survive. One summer, they had the opportunity to partner with the Boys & Girls Clubs of America for a summer program on their grounds. They didn't have to run the program, they just got to share their facility and volunteer from time to time and get to know some of the kids and leaders. Those relationships began to make their way into the Sunday morning prayers of the congregation. In time, a local newspaper ran a story about the summer partnership, and the congregation was thrilled to finally be part of good news in their community. Incredibly, even in just the beginning stages of fresh expression (listening, loving and serving, and building relationships) the spiritual vitality of this congregation began to increase.

Fresh expressions do not always directly add to your existing congregation's membership. But as the spiritual temperature of your congregation rises, visitors who are looking for a new church home will sense that there is something alive about this congregation. As they pick up on that vibe, they are more likely to stick around and want to be part of it. In this way, not only are participants and fresh expressions leadership teams being transformed, but so are existing congregations.

Amazement Seized All of Them!

For those who believe in God's mission, the decline of the church in North America is heartbreaking. But that is not the only story. Fresh expressions of church are right now being used by God's Spirit to engage people who would not likely connect with church in its traditional form. Through these small, simple, creative groups, people are finding their way to experiences of deep community that open pathways for them to encounter Jesus. The stories of genuine life transformation continue to emerge amidst these new faith communities. Just as Jesus did something profound in the life of the paralyzed man, his friends, and the whole community, so, too, is Jesus continuing to heal and restore lives and communities and congregations today. Fresh expressions is more than a church-growth strategy; it is the heartbeat of what God unleashed two thousand years ago as a gift to the world—Jesus communities infused with the power of God's wild and wonderful Spirit.

Discussion Questions

1. What is the difference between knowing about Jesus and experiencing Jesus? What is the difference between sharing about Jesus and helping people experience Jesus? As you reflect on these questions, is there anything that might need to change in the ways you engage in mission, outreach, and evangelism?

2. Research tells us that only 5 percent of Christians are actively discipling others.[11] How could the Fresh Expressions approach bump up that percentage in your congregation? And how might the life of your

congregation shift if more Christians were actively—and creatively—discipling others?

3. Where are you sensing boredom and lethargy in your congregation (if anywhere)? How might God be inviting you to stir some things up?

4. What do you long to see happening in and through your congregation?

A FRESH EXPRESSION STORY: THE SHELTER

A few congregation members stood around after a storm looking at the tree that had crashed through the detached garage of the parsonage. In the face of the wreckage, the pastor's wife looked up and said, "I don't think we should rebuild a garage. I think we should rebuild a gathering place for the community." That's how the Shelter was born. Through insurance claims and mission grants, but even more importantly, a vision to reach out to the greater community, a beautiful outdoor venue was erected where an old garage had once stood. It would become a place where musicians flocked to play concerts because it was a great vibe in a unique setting. Thursday Night Live at the Shelter began as music, a meal, and a message, and throughout the community, you could hear people inviting their friends to "meet me at the Shelter." Soon, the Shelter was becoming a hub of connection bringing together a diverse assortment of people and musicians. One day, a local came and sat under a tree, keeping a distance, but watching what was happening. She returned the following Thursday and the Thursday after that, never participating, just listening to the music a step away. Finally, one night she approached someone and was ready for a conversation. She admitted she was living in her car, addicted to meth, and estranged from her family. Instead of judgment, she found embrace. As they helped her through the immediate rough patch, she shared honestly, "I'm not going to quit today, but I am going to quit."

Today, she is four years clean, recently received employee of the month, and has discovered she is actually loved by Jesus. She will tell you today that the Shelter saved her life. This child of God would not likely have made her way to a traditional church, but a community of music, food, and love opened the door to new life, both literally and spiritually. From a storm-wrecked garage to life-changing community, that's the beautiful work of the Holy Spirit through fresh expressions of church.

CHAPTER SIX

THE STORY CONTINUES
How Can Your Church Get Started?

As dramatic changes are occurring in our world at an ever-quickening pace, God is beckoning the church into God's mission field all around us. So how do we get started?

Cultivate a Missional Culture

In many congregations, the first step in starting a fresh expression of church will be to help your people begin to turn their attention to the world around them. Pastors and leaders can help people inside the church become attuned to the types of people the church is not reaching. Get as creative as you like with this. Perhaps you can set up a whiteboard and invite the congregation to add phrases and descriptions of people and subcultures who, for whatever reason, are not connecting with your church. Challenge them to get a little more thoughtful than their knee-jerk reaction of "young families." Suggestions like travel sports families, nearby residents, marathon runners, recent immigrants, factory workers, and so on.

Then begin praying for these people groups. Pastors and leaders can foster conversations that help the congregation imagine creative, intentional ways they could potentially engage those who may never come through their church doors.

Prayer-walking is another great way to begin to turn your attention to the neighborhood and community around you. Walking your community and letting the places, situations, and people shape your praying is a powerful way to begin seeing what God wants you to see and meditating on God's dreams for the community. Talk with people and listen to their hopes and dreams and stories. Notice where God is already at work. Take note of where there is grief, pain, and need—where there is a gap between the kingdom of God and what you are seeing right in front of you. Pray silently as you walk. Pray conversationally as you walk. Perhaps God may even stir you to ask someone you just encountered if it would be okay for you to pray with them. Prayer-walking is a powerful practice for fostering a more missional culture.

Leverage the vision or the values that launched your congregation or your denomination. Remembering the passions, courage, and faith that was a driving force in the early days can create a motivating throughline for your congregation. "We've always cared about those who feel forgotten" or "We have a long history of mentoring young people."

Pastors and Bible study leaders can do some teaching and preaching around missional texts in Scripture. Help your congregations to see that God has always been pursuing those who have wandered off and those who have been left out. This God sent Jesus into the world to bring the kingdom near, and Jesus sends us into the world to continue this mission.

Finally, be the kind of leader that embodies the culture you would like to cultivate in your congregation. When other people in your church see you spending more time with your neighbors, hosting people to dinner, building relationships with people being served through your church's mission projects, and more, you are setting an example. That example shifts priorities and slowly changes a culture.

Find Those Who Share the Vision

When you share the vision of fresh expressions, who do you notice leaning forward with excitement? Who is coming to you with ideas? When you start talking about fresh expression possibilities, both inside and outside your church, who lights up and wants to get involved? Who is unexpectedly revealing a need in your community or a possibility for partnership? These are all signals of people who share the vision.

Invite these people into further conversation over a meal or a cup of coffee. Dream together and pray together. Grab a few copies of a Fresh Expressions resource and read and reflect on it together.

Consider these questions:

1. What do you love? What are the interests, passions, or people that make you come alive? For example, maybe you love working out or you love woodworking.

2. What do you know? What are some skills, talents, or areas of expertise that you have. Maybe you know a lot about working with special-needs children or you have artistic talent.

3. Who do you know? What are the people groups or networks with whom you are already connected? For example, you are involved in the local Little League community or a group of gamers or you regularly hang out with classic car enthusiasts.

4. What do you have? Do you have a great backyard with a firepit? Do you have access to a commercial kitchen?

These questions, along with listening in your community, will give you clues to where you might be best positioned to try some fresh expression experiments.

Work with What You've Got

Many congregations are already serving locally. Perhaps you are already feeding the hungry in your community. Maybe you have a long-time partnership with a local school. Or you are already filling some of the needs that you've encountered in your community. This is a beautiful thing.

But is it possible that you could invest more deeply in building relationships as you serve? You already have natural connections with these groups of people. What could it look like for you to add incarnational elements to what you are already doing? How could you build community among those you are serving and those who are volunteering?

Sometimes God isn't inviting you to start something brand-new. Sometimes God is inviting you to deepen what you are already doing.

Start Simple

Fresh expressions don't tend to start with three-year strategic plans with multi-million-dollar budgets. They start with disciples who care about those who don't yet know the joy of life with God; they find a friend or two to join them; they find practical ways to love and serve and build friendships; and they share their thoughts and feelings about Jesus as a natural part of a life of everyday faith. As they go, they discover that some are becoming more curious about faith, or even coming to faith, and they begin to encourage that group to form a Christian community right where they are.

Start with a simple experiment. The friends of the paralyzed man started with an idea and a simple experiment. *Let's try to get this pallet on the roof!* What are one or two simple experiments you could try to begin to connect, love, and serve people God is placing on your heart?

A FRESH EXPRESSION STORY: EMERGE

Rebecca served a small-town church as a local pastor. The church, like the town, was small, but Rebecca invited a few others from the congregation to start prayer-walking with her. As they prayer-walked for several months, Rebecca began to get a picture of Joshua marching around the walls of Jericho and the walls falling. Some of the people from the church began to get impatient, asking, "When are we going to *do* something?" But Rebecca and the team continued to listen and pray. As they persisted, God began to make them acutely aware of just how many teenagers seemed to be lost and drifting, with nothing to do and no church connection. The Spirit opened their hearts to these young people and they began to sense that now God was asking them to do something. Knowing that the church building would be a barrier to connecting with young people in their town, Rebecca and her team pursued permission to use the community center. There, they started convening opportunities for teenagers to gather for gaming, fun activities, and connection. Meanwhile, church members gave themselves over to a candlelight prayer walk, circling the town and praying for the Holy Spirit to be poured out upon every person in the community. In a matter of a few months a newly formed youth band was taught a few worship songs, and a Thursday night worship service began to unfold right there in the community center. A meal was served by volunteers, the band played, and someone shared a creative message about Jesus. Young people started to ask to be baptized, and surprisingly, so did a seventy-five-year-old volunteer. Just like Rebecca had pictured in those early prayer walks, she was now seeing the walls of hardened hearts crumbling. One small church in one small community started to pay attention to how God was inviting them out of their sanctuary and into their community to do something different. And through their faithfulness, God has done more than they could have ever asked or imagined.

Discussion Questions

1. What are some ideas from this chapter that resonated as you consider cultivating a missional culture in your congregation?

2. What is one mission your congregation is already doing? How might you deepen what you are already doing by living out the Fresh Expression journey there?

3. Are there two or three people who are coming to mind that you might want to gather for a conversation about fresh expressions? Who are they? Can you text them and invite them to coffee or dinner right now?

4. What is your next step?

How Can Fresh Expressions North America Help?

We have a variety of resources and trainings to support a variety of needs. If you are an individual sensing a call to start a fresh expression of church, you may want to explore Pioneer Cohorts and our practical resources developed with pioneers in mind.[12] Fresh Expressions coaches can help you discern your call and help you think through your team and your next steps. And our emerging community of pioneers are finding strength and support through connecting points being convened by Fresh Expression practitioners.[13]

If you are a team working on a fresh expression initiative, team coaching and peer gatherings are available to provide guidance and healthy intention as you work together in a common mission.

If you are a pastor or leader in a local church, Fresh Expressions can bring training and consultation to your church to catalyze a vision for fresh expressions of church and provide support as you develop your local approach. In addition, Fresh Expressions provides free webinars, podcasts, resources, and more to continue to give you the tools, stories, and thought leadership that will reinforce and enhance your vision casting efforts with your congregation.

If you are a denominational leader, there are ways to partner with Fresh Expressions to host regional training events, develop regional strategies, and resource your pioneering leaders.

If you are particularly interested in starting a dinner church or other meal-centered gathering Fresh Expressions has a team offering specialized training on this approach. Considering a hobby or recreation as a connecting point for your fresh expression initiative? Fresh Expressions has practitioners experienced in this arena. Thinking about your home as a center point for mission? Fresh Expressions has trainers with experience in this modality.

If you need prayer support, Fresh Expressions offers ways for you to meet and pray with an intercessor, resources for prayer, and training in prayer for mission.

Find out about all these resources, join the mailing list, connect to videos/blogs/podcasts/app and more through our website: www.freshexpressions.com.

A Challenge and a Prayer

This is the moment that God is calling the church to take a step of faith. Imagine if there were a dinner church in every town. Imagine if there were an activated pioneer in every congregation. Imagine if every one of your congregation's mission projects became missional communities. I think we, like that crowd in Luke's account, would be seized by amazement as revival begins to unfold.

That revival starts with one faithful step, trusting the promises that God is already out ahead of you.

Two thousand years ago, Jesus sent his disciples out into all the towns and villages where he was asking them to go, inviting them to immerse themselves into the homes and rhythms of those places, sharing peace and receiving the hospitality of those who welcomed them. Today, he is inviting you to do the same.

Gracious God, Jesus has promised that those who follow him will be where he is. So make us faithful followers. Give us the grace and the courage to follow wherever he leads and the heart to love as he loves, trusting in the promise that you are with us always, even to the end of the age. Amen.

FREQUENTLY ASKED QUESTIONS

Is a fresh expression just another way to refer to a small group or Bible Study?

While a fresh expression might have some similarities, it is really meant to be more. It is a community of people following Jesus together, committed to more than just meeting together and studying Scripture and seeking to be more than just a social club. Formed by Scripture and commitment to pursue the Jesus way in community, this group is being shaped into a community marked by sacrificial service, authentic relationships, and spiritual transformation.

What's the difference between a traditional mission/outreach and a fresh expression?

The difference is in the posture. A mission or outreach is often ministry that is *to* or *for* people. A fresh expression is about forming community *with* people. This ministry of "with-ness" is the key to fresh expressions and can be applied to missions you are already doing to begin to facilitate a shift from transactional encounters to incarnational community.

What if our congregation doesn't have any pioneers?

Trust me . . . you do. Pioneers come in all shapes, ages, and temperaments. When you begin to help people see that they can do what they love, do it with others and with God, there are some who will suddenly come alive. "I love to play Mahjong! Are you saying that it would give God joy for me to start a Mahjong group and follow the Holy Spirit there? I'm in!" Remember, you are not looking for someone to start a 500-member church plant; you are looking for people who are open to naturally connecting with people in the everyday intersections of life and living out relationship and discipleship right there.

How do you equip laity to lead fresh expressions?

Fresh Expressions North America offers plenty of resources to support laity. Put a resource in the hands of your pioneers (*Becoming Church* by Luke Edwards is a good choice) and start meeting together to talk about what they are reading and learning. Help them discern the people, place, or passion that will be the focal point of their mission and encourage and pray for them as they shape out next steps. If there are particular nuances of your theological stream that would be important for the grounding of this mission, have a conversation about your unique theological identity and dialogue about how best to apply those distinctives in a postmodern mission context. Provide the resources for your laity to attend a Pioneer Cohort to access both training and peer-to-peer encouragement. Most importantly, ongoing relational support—spiritual mentorship, encouragement, and feedback—will be the key to empowered laity.

How do you navigate the sacraments in laity-led fresh expressions?

This will look different within different denominational settings. Find the people in your denominational stream who can help you creatively negotiate the guidelines that may exist in your particular tradition. In some traditions, laity can become credentialed within particular offices of the church to share the sacraments. In others, clergy will need to be present. In others, already-consecrated elements can be served. This is where the connection with your inherited church can be a beautiful partnership, as clergy who may have only baptized new believers in a church sanctuary setting find themselves invited to assist at the riverside, a backyard pool, or a barn.

How does a fresh expression deepen and mature?

As people are coming to faith, they are also helping to shape what is becoming. Don't neglect drawing the group into conversations around what this emerging community should look like. Be careful of importing your own agenda into the rhythms of the community and allow others to take an ownership and investment in what is developing. Let them give voice to ideas for prayer, worship, faith exploration, mission, and mutual care. If this is going to be a Jesus-shaped community in a particular context, those who are part of that context need mentors to provide guardrails that reflect the way of Jesus but also need permission to help shape the mission.

Our church is already tired and struggling to find volunteers. What if we don't have the bandwidth for adding fresh expressions to the mix?

Fresh expressions are about shifting from primarily maintenance mode to mission. You don't need the buy-in from the whole church; you need a few who are willing to try low-cost experiments on the edges and discover what God can do when we step out in faith. Continuing to default to maintenance mode will not likely change the trajectory of "tired and struggling." The more important question to ask is: "What if we don't do this?" And, remember, fresh expressions are most naturally formed as a deepening or embracing of what you are already doing. Where do you already spend your time? Where are you already doing mission? What are your hobbies, interests, or passions? Focus more on what you are already doing and less on adding something brand-new.

What is dinner church?

Dinner church is a stream within the Fresh Expressions movement that is centered around the Jesus table. It is simply a community dinner where all gather together for a lavish meal, great hospitality, good conversation, a story about Jesus, and life-on-life connection. As strangers become friends around a dinner table, Christ is present. Often focused on connecting with people in economically challenged neighborhoods or young people longing for authentic community, dinner church is an easily replicable form of church that any congregation—no matter your size or location—can do. Find out more and get practical resources for dinner church at www.dinner church.com.

What is Messy Church?

Messy Church is a stream within the Fresh Expressions movement that helps families not connected to any church discover Jesus through intergenerational play, curiosity, creativity, food, and fun. More than a children's ministry, Messy Church is creating an inclusive, joyful community in which people of all ages can experience a God of hospitality and unconditional love. Find out more and get practical resources for Messy Church at https:// messychurchusa.org/.

What is Church @ Play?

Church @ Play is a stream within the Fresh Expressions movement that helps people imagine forming fresh expressions of church in the midst of shared hobbies, interests, and recreation. From hiking to gaming to yoga to painting—and more—new Christian communities can emerge among the very things you love to do. Find stories of these kinds of affinity-based fresh expressions at our website.

What is House Church?

House Church is a stream within the Fresh Expressions movement that reimagines the home as a center point for mission. Through small, home-based gatherings, neighbors are connecting with neighbors. Through networks of House Churches, traditional churches that were primarily program-based are finding new ways to connect with their neighbors through home-based gatherings. Find stories and resources for these kinds of Christian communities at our website: www.fresh expressions.com.

GLOSSARY OF TERMS

Blended Ecology of Church—a new form of local congregation that arises from fresh expressions of church in symbiotic relationship with inherited forms of church

Contextual—attentive to and shaped by the setting and culture of the mission

Inherited Church—existing or established forms of church; this is the form of church with which most of us are familiar—gathering on Sunday mornings and living out the enduring marks of the church; they are deep and rich reservoirs of the great inheritance of faith which we have received

Missional—sent into the world to embody the missionary nature of God and God's church rather than viewing missions as one activity among many

Mixed Ecology of Church—the coexistence of both a traditional (inherited) form of church and one or more fresh expression initiatives alongside that particular inherited church

Permission-Giver—a person of influence who can leverage that influence to cast vision, offer support to pioneers, and give permission for a Fresh Expressions movement to take root

Person of Peace—a person from the broader community who serves as a bridge between a Fresh Expression and the community; this person can often open doors of relationship or resource that can bless the mission

Pioneer—a person who leads a Fresh Expression; tends to have gifts of compassion, connecting with people, infectious faith, and an adventurous spirit

Post-Christian—a period or society where Christianity is no longer the main religion

Postmodern—a late twentieth-century movement characterized by broad skepticism, subjectivism, and relativism

Supporter—typically not the front-line leader, a person who will bless a fresh expression initiative through prayer, support, and practical hands-on help

Third Place—places where people spend time between home (first place) and work (second place); they are places where we exchange ideas, have a good time, and build relationship

NOTES

1. "Fewer Congregations Are Growing," 2020 Faith Communities Today Survey, Hartford Institute for Religious Research, 2021, Hartford Seminary, CT, https://hirr.hartfordinternational.edu/wp-content/uploads/2024/10/Report-on-the-2020-Faith-Communities-Today-Survey-of-Nondenominational-and-Independent-Churches.pdf.

2. Ryan Burge, "How Many Nones Are There?" November 9, 2023, Data: Cooperative Election Study, 2020, https://www.graphsaboutreligion.com/p/how-many-nones-are-there.

3. Ryan Burge, *The Nones: Where They Came From, Who They Are, and Where They Are Going*, Second Edition (Fortress Press, 2023).

4. @Ryan Burge, "Age Distribution of Protestant Traditions," X, February 1, 2023, Data: Cooperative Election Study, 2020, https://x.com/ryanburge/status/1620913806003286019?s=61&t=_nUBDWqu9Nm6ip3TPGYrqA&mx=2.

5. *Mission-Shaped Church: Church Planting and Fresh Expressions of Church in a Changing Context* (Church House Publishing, 2004), 100, emphasis added; Church of England. *The Declaration of Assent.* Available at: https://www.churchofengland.org/prayer -and-worship/worship-texts-and-resources/common -worship/ministry/declaration-assent#na.

6. Bill Bishop, *The Big Sort: Why the Clustering of Like-Minded America Is Tearing Us Apart* (Mariner Books, 2009).

7. Bob Smietana, "Two-Thirds of Churchgoers Have Invited Someone to Church," Lifeway, July 12, 2018, https://news.lifeway.com/2018/07/12/two-thirds-of -churchgoers-have-invited-someone-to-church/.

8. Eugene Peterson, *A Long Obedience in the Same Direction: Discipleship in an Instant Society* (IVP, 2000).

9. "The Peace Prayer of Saint Francis," https://www .journeywithjesus.net/poemsandprayers/554-saint -francis-of-assisi.

10. Ray Oldenburg, *The Great Good Place: Café's, Coffee Shops, Bookstores, Bars, Hair Salons and Other Hangouts at the Heart of a Community*, 3rd ed. (Marlowe and Company, 1989).

11. "Two in Five Christians Are Not Engaged in Discipleship," Barna Group, January 26, 2022, https:// www.barna.com/research/christians-discipleship -community/.

12. For more information about Pioneer Cohorts, see https://freshexpressions.com/training/pioneer-cohort.

13. For more information about Fresh Expression leaders, see https://freshexpressions.com/regional-church-leaders. Explore the FreshExpressions.com website to discover more details, training, and resources.

Printed by Libri Plureos GmbH in Hamburg,
Germany